Organic Gardening Without Poisons

Organic Gardening
Without Poisons

Hamilton Tyler

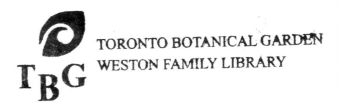

TORONTO BOTANICAL GARDEN
WESTON FAMILY LIBRARY

VAN NOSTRAND REINHOLD COMPANY
NEW YORK   CINCINNATI   TORONTO   LONDON   MELBOURNE

Drawings by Adrián Martinez, Don Giannoni, and Charles Hoeppner

Van Nostrand Reinhold Company Regional Offices:
New York   Cincinnati   Chicago   Millbrae   Dallas

Van Nostrand Reinhold Company International Offices:
London   Toronto   Melbourne

Published by Van Nostrand Reinhold Company
450 West 33rd Street, New York, N.Y. 10001

Published simultaneously in Canada by
Van Nostrand Reinhold Company Ltd.

Contents

Introduction: Man and Nature

The clear river you swam in as a child is now a filthy ditch; the bowl of fruits that was once an object of desire is now a source of doubt—have they really been washed well enough, or is there a spray residue that may do anything from changing chromosomes to causing a malignancy? Recently, a friend told me his family liked birds and were very sorry when the spray for his black-eyed peas laid the songbirds out in windrows—it killed them all. He wouldn't have done it, he said, but the spray was new and he didn't know. Nor did he know the human effects.

Man has lived on the earth for a period as long as two million years. For most of that time, he was a successful and well-adapted species, following nature's seasons and harvesting crops. Contrary to what we were once taught, this life in quest of fruit, berries, and game was not one of desperation—it was rather one of modest abundance, with the limiting factor not food supply, but food preservation.

There is at present little harmony of man with nature. Early men followed nature's ways and its seasons with a sharp eye. Primitive man always searched for signs—how should he behave when faced with the mysterious forces in weather, vegetation, and the animal life about him? The cry of a bird, the lay of a leaf—all of these could be taken as signs. Careful observation would provide the clues to the requirements of nature.

Today, we have lost sight of man and his environment. We are too quick to spray chemicals when we see an insect, not realizing that the very same chemical may kill the predator that keeps the insect under control. We are too quick to poison the air and kill birds that eat insects by the score and are a gardener's friend. We are, in short, moving too rapidly in the wrong direction; we are eliminating natural beauty and the natural balance between man and nature. In order to go forward, I think we must first go backward.

First of all, we should look again for signs and directions, just as primitive man did. Any garden is a small paradise. And more miraculous, anyone can create a garden where none existed before. Any gardener who is going to copy nature's methods should know something about the basic processes. All life is dependent on plant life, and when we start using sprays to counteract the ill effects of other sprays in our gardens we are contributing in some degree to going in the wrong direction. You are not alone in quest for beauty and color in your garden; there are millions. As a group, why don't we go in the right direction and use nature's ways? And at the same time we will be doing our own individual part to remedy an already deplorable situation.

The health of a plant is a complex matter, depending upon such factors as vigorous growth and inbred resistance to particular diseases. There also are other important things that may be protecting a plant. The bacteria which thrive in organically rich matter secrete substances which destroy soil-born disease organisms. Fungi produce antibiotics such as pencillin, and these may control plant disease or increase resistance. While a gardener can never be specific about events in this micro-world, it is a comfort to know that many of them are working for us, *if we will allow them to*. If we do not kill them with chemicals.

I have seen dozens of beautiful organic gardens. They are not, certainly, completely free from insects—any more than the average person is free for a lifetime from colds.

Every garden is a kind of small paradise that shelters us from the dreary wastes of concrete and asphalt that abound on all sides. A garden provides beauty for the eye, contentment for the mind, and often some delights for the palate. No gardener should poison this place of refuge. With good practices he should not have to do so.

1. Pesticides Against Countrysides

We all want beautiful surroundings. We all want pretty gardens and attractive landscaping. Whether large or small, in city or country, the garden is becoming more and more a priceless commodity—that small piece of nature that is our very own.

In an effort to guard our sylvan settings, we have been led to believe we must protect trees and shrubs, flowers and hedges from insects by the use of pesticide sprays. Yet applying sprays on plants has caused more havoc than the insects themselves could ever manage. The effect sprays have had on our ecology is now the subject of headlines every day as more and more wildlife is lost.

Today we are trying to save what land we have left. And one way to contribute to this conservation is to garden in harmony with nature. Every garden counts; though each may not seem significant by itself, it becomes vitally important when multiplied by millions.

The idea that a partial ban on DDT is a solution to our ecology problems is erroneous. Even if we completely ban the use of DDT there are a host of other poisons in use—aldrin, dieldrin, heptachlor, BHC, and others. Any of the first three mentioned will be as deadly when spread at the rate of two to three pounds per acre as is DDT at twenty-five pounds per acre. Furthermore, they are more hazardous to warm-blooded animals, including ourselves.

So the war is far from won in the battle with the people who manufacture poisons. You only win a skirmish or perhaps settle for a draw. They will be back with new weapons and new arguments. The banning of DDT in a few states is no real answer; it should not be taken as any real victory or as a reason for complacency.

In the meantime, as individuals we can contribute to conservation and ecology by banning all poisons from our gardens, and by tilling the soil so the balance of nature can be restored. We should have some knowledge of poisons and how to have lovely gardens without them. We must know what we are fighting for. If we are prepared, perhaps we can win.

CHLORINATED HYDROCARBONS

All poisons are toxic by definition, but with some, the lethal effects and side effects last for a long time. By lasting, they make it possible to build up a complete chain of death and desolation. There was a time when rainwater was the very symbol of purity, but no more. Rain now often falls with its component of dieldrin, BHC, and the DDT group. These gather on dust particles and then are deposited in some distant part of the country.

Opposite
Mill Tilly's charming garden in Mill Valley flourishes with iris, flax, and Chinese forget-me-nots. It has been tended for over forty years without poisons of any kind whatsoever. *Richard F. Conrat photo*

Sprays applied in Texas are found to fall out in a rain over Cleveland, Ohio. The persistent poisons known as chlorinated hydrocarbons can make such long journeys without losing any of their toxic quality. Rainwater drenches the landscape, runs off in concentrated amounts through streams and rivers, fills up in bays, and deposits itself at the mouths of rivers. Some of the toxic content is lost slowly, but it still builds up because it is chemically stable, or, in a few cases, it breaks down into something even more toxic.

What are the names of these persistent poisons that we will still have to face even if DDT is stricken from the list? The worst of these chlorinated hydrocarbons belong to the aldrin-toxaphene group. The important members of this destructive clan are aldrin, endrin, dieldrin, heptachlor, and toxaphene.

Some people argue that the last of these, toxaphene, is not as bad as the first four; possibly, but all too much of it is already in the soil and atmosphere, since farmers use it about as much as DDT. We will soon be finding out what particular damage it does.

A second group is popular in home garden sprays but is not so widely used in agriculture. Home sprays can't do as much damage as commercial and massive applications, but one should keep in mind that it is the *private* car—in large numbers—that has made our air almost unbreathable. In this group are lindane, chlordane, kelthane, and Tedion. Yet another member—methoxychlor—is said to be less toxic to warm-blooded animals than DDT. Since, in this negative way, it has the best reputation of the group, you will see it listed more and more often on home garden spray labels. It is largely used against caterpillars and beetles, but, in later chapters, we will discuss better ways of controlling these pests.

There are minor members of this persistent poison train, such as bulan, prolan, kepone, and eulan. They are lesser cards that will likely be shuffled into the deck because of their very obscurity. Watch for their names in the small print on spray-can labels.

All of these persistent poisons have a virtue which turns out to be a vice: they last. In theory, that is a good thing, because the bug that comes along next week instead of the day you chose to spray will also be killed. Unfortunately, so will all the beneficial insects that pass that way, even weeks later.

The poison issue is not simply a matter of killing off the parasites and predators that keep one pest in check. Researchers at the Riverside campus of the University of California have found that DDT has a stimulative effect on mite populations. Their conjecture is that these chemicals increase the food value of the host plant—for the mite. This means, more broadly, that we don't really know what we are doing when we apply these chemical poisons. It is ironic to think we may be feeding the pests we are trying to control and at the same time destroying all of their enemies. As a result, it becomes increasingly difficult to build up a garden of lovely flowers and shrubs.

Side effects—the polite phrase for unexpected results—sometimes bring direct economic losses. When money is involved, someone usually takes count of the loss, but the value of wildlife is not something that the ordinary man can put on one side of his ledger or the other. California rice fields are sprayed with dieldrin from airplanes; the residue floats as a film on the surface of any shallow water. Wading birds, such as egrets and herons, are killed by this film in the dosages that farmers are advised to use.

Toads and frogs are particularly susceptible to this group of poisons because they have a permeable skin and absorb toxic material directly. Only one pound of DDT applied to an acre will kill many of them, and a slightly higher amount will eliminate amphibians entirely. The spray residue settles in the shallow water at the edges of streams or ditches and covers vernal pools. These are the places where amphibians breed. So we lose these insect-eating friends.

In the spring, insect-eating birds that appear in gardens and are vital to a total environment are often victims of these poisons. Any perching bird is trapped by its blindness and is drenched where it sits. DDT will kill adult birds if applied at the rate of five pounds per acre, and other chlorinated hydrocarbons, such as dieldrin, will kill them when applied at only a fraction of that amount.

Sprays may be applied at various seasons, but spring is certain to be one of them. In the spring these birds are nesting, having chosen an orchard for a site since it provides insect food. The baby birds are naked, and exposed to whatever comes along, which, too often, is death.

These persistent sprays also affect the earthworm population. Earthworms eat their way through the soil containing poison residues; they also eat the fallen leaves that have been sprayed. The residue is concentrated in the earthworm's body and may or may not kill it, depending upon the amount. But if a toad or a bird eats a number of these worms, the amount will of course be multiplied by the number of worms eaten, and the result is a kind of toxic time bomb. Fish and shrimp are now often acting as similar living bombs in the ocean ecology.

HERBICIDES AND DEFOLIANTS

Everyone loves a lovely lawn and detests weeds —so, in answer to the public clamor for a weed-free garden, we got herbicides and defoliants. They are extremely powerful.

My first realization of how potent these poisons can be came when a county chemical truck drove along my road. A trickle ran down a gopher hole and made its way fifty feet or more to my lawn. It not only killed a patch the size of a washtub, but after three seasons no grass would grow back, and I was forced to dig out the patch and discard that soil.

Some of these herbicides are phytotoxic—that is, poisonous to plants. Others function as "growth regulators." Some of the phytotoxic materials are too effective to be used on crops, though they may be used on roadsides. Bromacil and simazine break down slowly, and they may sterilize the soil completely for as long as three years. Diuron is also a long-term soil sterilant.

Growth regulators sound like a more gentle approach until you look into the matter; those such as picloram and dicamba can seldom be used because they kill all broad-leaved plants unselectively. It even says so on the can. They also last long enough to destroy or damage the next crop of greenery. Some of the "growth regulators" are hormone sprays. Among these, some have the effect of increasing the reproduction rate of aphids. This result was pointed out by the honest scientists who keep testing the effects of new poisons.

Again, these side effects point up the fact that most of us don't really know what we are doing when we apply these chemicals. A particular hormone spray increases the number of aphids; but the use of 2,4-D, one of the most commonly used herbicides, has the opposite effect on ladybugs and their larvae. It kills some larvae outright, it deforms others, and it delays the onset of pupation.

These sprays which have been sold as labor-saving servants for man have again turned around to increase the gardener's enemies and destroy many of his friends, and with them, the garden. More aphids and fewer ladybugs are not the answer. There is no need to go through the long list of chemical names under which these herbicides are classed, nor the longer list of trade names under which they are sold to the public.

The point to remember is that when these compounds break down, they become part of the soil until there may come a time when nothing will grow in your garden. In some cases, the chemists shuffle the deck and point out that the herbicide breaks down into a fertilizer—on paper, that is. The honest scientists are willing to admit that they never know all the factors involved or what side effects there may be, so the layman should share their doubt and ponder it.

Certain chemicals of either natural or synthetic derivation are known to have a doubling effect on the chromosomes when they penetrate a normal cell. Cancer consists in doubling the chromosomes in a few cells.

Growth-regulating herbicides work by penetrating plant cells, where they either rearrange or destroy chromosomes. That raises the point as to what may happen to animal cells when sprayed residues are eaten. There is now evidence that baby chicks may be killed by eating corn from a field sprayed with herbicides like 2,4,5-T.

Chromosomes contain the genes—the code-bearers that direct reproductive cells. Recently, some bad messages have been sent. A Bionetics Institute report has shown that rats and mice fed a minimum dosage of 2,4,5-T will produce 39 percent abnormal fetuses.

The effect of these chemicals on human animals is not yet proved, but do we need such dubious methods to get rid of weeds? Rather than being a garden help, herbicides could very well be another step into a hopelessly poisoned world.

SYSTEMICS AND OTHER POISONS

There are many other chemical compounds with toxic powers. Systemics have been on the market for a number of years with much fanfare from garden-magazine advertisements. Yet no one knows at all the ultimate effects of using the systemics. The names of this group are Di-syston and Meta-systox-R. These are not sprayed on plants like other toxins but are "planted" in the ground around the plants. Growing things draw them up through roots and vascular systems and store the poisons in each plant cell.

The concept seems a step backward even though it will kill sucking insects. To being with, you can't possibly use these on food plants, nor should you use them in your garden, since these chemicals are highly toxic to humans and animals. The systemics control only a few insects—such as aphids, leafhoppers, and mealybugs—and any decent gardener can surely control these without recourse to chemical warfare.

There are still other poisons: carbaryl, called Sevin in the trade, is one. Commercial sprayers tell me it is not very effective. That may be a good thing or a bad thing, but it has one side effect that is certain. Chemically, it is related to the carbamates used as herbicides. In use, it is particularly destructive to honeybees. If you grow a small orchard or a large one, honeybees will do more pollinating for your plot than the wind will.

Now that you have read this gloomy list, perhaps you are ready to ask: "Enough—what can I do as an alternative?" There *is* a better way to garden or farm which doesn't demand blind experimentation with one new poison after another— and its details are briefly outlined in the chapters that follow.

The author tending his garden. No insecticides or sprays are used on his property. *Joyce R. Wilson photo*

13

2. The Soil Around Us

Ordinarily we think of earth as something under our feet, dusty in summer and muddy in winter. For a foundation on which to build a house, we need only a stable base; but for a garden, however modest in size or design, we need not just earth but topsoil—and our success depends upon its richness.

More often than not, potential garden soil is less than perfect. We may have to start a garden on sand or clay. Gravel can cause a great deal of trouble, while gumbo, a very fine-grained soil, presents different problems. Because it is these soil conditions that trouble us from the very beginning, we often think of the problem of soil as one of physical structure. Structure is important, but actually it is only one factor in a wider reality.

SOIL AND MICROBES

Soil contains a vast world of life. We are familiar with the friendly earthworm and the unfriendly cutworm; but beyond this visible world lies a much larger group of living things, microscopic in size. These tiny plants and animals are called microbes. There are many microscopic animals in topsoil, but an almost incredible number of bacteria—which are microscopic plants. It takes five hundred billion bacteria to weigh a pound, and in each acre of topsoil there are from thirty to forty pounds of these plant microbes. Plant microorganisms have no green matter and are unable to produce any food for themselves. Some of them are parasitic; most of them are saprophytic, which means that they live by digesting dead organic matter.

All members of this underground life-world relate in a dynamic equilibrium. After each change, a new rough harmony or balance always returns. This is true because each soil organism fits into a scheme larger than that of its own survival. The balance returns quickly, if man has not poisoned the soil and thrown the systems into disarray. Toxic mixes of chemicals produce a chain reaction in the life-world below us, and some of the results have proved to be both long-lasting and disastrous.

WATER

The functions of water are quite complex. Water supplies things and at the same time it does things. There is a mixture of the living and the mechanical in the function of water. Soil holds water, but not like a vase—the moisture needs to be kept up where the roots can reach it. Since plant cells and ultimately all organic material are made up of elaborations of hydrogen and oxygen combined with carbon, water is a basic building block for any living thing.

On another level, water is a solvent. When plant-food minerals are free, they are dissolved or

Opposite
Good soil with lots of humus is black and crumbly; it promotes excellent growth in plants.

Above
The difference between good soil and clay soil is seen in this photograph; the spaded soil has a good texture and is black, the clay soil is caked and gray. *O. M. Scott & Co. photo*

Opposite
A clay soil will not produce healthy plants; it is hard and heavy, and air and water cannot move through it easily. *USDA photo*

suspended in water, and plants can then draw this nourishment into their systems. Water also carries off plant waste products as it evaporates from the surfaces of leaves.

Water behavior depends on the structure of the soil. When you water a sandy bed and come back in a few hours to find it completely dry, you might say that the drainage is too sharp. In a sandy soil, not only will roots wither but the soluble foods in the soil will leach away. The soluble food matter in the topsoil drains downward with the moisture content. Sand is like a sieve which allows water to run out through the open spaces. Clay and adobe, on the other hand, have no small openings or pores. Water, then, must find its way through occasional cracks. Penetration is at best uneven, and at worst water may pool up on the surface.

Good soil has a high organic content. This organic material is called humus, and it improves the water-holding capacity of any topsoil. Organic matter has the physical ability to hold and distribute moisture evenly. You can observe this when firewood is left out in the rain. Water is absorbed quickly, distributed evenly, and dispersed slowly.

AIR

Air circulates through the soil and is necessary to the life there. This underworld air is similar to that which we breathe, except that the gases exist in different proportions and densities.

A soil atmosphere must make its way through pores, so we try to keep a good tilth or looseness in our garden soil. A friable, or crumbly, soil assures a good circulation of necessary gases. While the green and growing parts of plants above ground give off oxygen, the same gas is needed by the roots below. The all-important inert gas nitrogen enters the soil through these pores also, and is then transformed into usable plant food.

17

Tilling is necessary so air and water can penetrate the soil to reach plants. *Gilson Bros. photo*

HOW SOIL ORIGINATES AND MAINTAINS ITSELF

Soil begins as rock. For, surprisingly, lifeless stones and living things have much in common. The same minerals and many chemical compounds find their way from rocks, to soil, to plants, and then to animals. Like living things, rocks are also subject to decay, and that is a good thing. This decay releases minerals and starts the building of topsoil.

Rock decay begins with mechanical grinding and shifting. Cracks appear here and there, and larger pieces break up into smaller ones in ever diminishing size. Chemical decay begins when water, oxygen, and carbon dioxide enter cracks. Minerals released by crumbling produce new chemical compounds, and these, with the help of cold and heat, further transform rocks.

The gardener has nothing to do with these age-old processes; they take place over too long a span of time. But many other processes do concern the gardener. Roots physically divide not only large rocks but also small particles of soil. Decaying vegetation supplies food for the soil organisms, and these in turn produce chemical changes in the soil. Microbes generate sulfuric and carbonic acids, which further the decay of rocks and release their mineral content. Even the diligent earthworm can digest rock particles along with organic matter. The combination is then distributed in the soil in the form of rich castings.

To understand the living world in the topsoil, we have to take a brief glance at the world above. Green plants take inorganic elements from both earth and sky. They take the shower of sunlight, and, in the magic alembic of the plant cell, this light energy is changed by chlorophyll into chemical energy. Water is combined with carbon dioxide and transformed into sugars, which are in turn the food of the life essence—protoplasm.

When the plant has completed its growth, it returns to the soil in the form of organic matter. Both bacteria and fungi are litter-decomposers which return these values to the soil and also create new ones. Any healthy living plant will have extracted from soil and air the right balance of minerals for maintaining its growth. Different plants have slightly different mineral requirements, but, when combined and returned to the soil through the action of microorganisms, this organic matter will supply everything necessary for another cycle of growth.

IMPROVING SOIL STRUCTURE

Soil can always be amended, in a mechanical way, by adding various types of rock or sand. River sand is often very cheap, but it takes a great deal of labor to spread the number of tons needed to loosen a clay soil. Greensand and rock phosphate are both pulverized rocks. They have the physical effects of sand, plus a fertilizer value which helps to make the effort worthwhile. There are lighter materials made of exploded minerals. Perlite is a kind of volcanic glass which forms seedlike balls, while vermiculite is an exploded mica. The latter has the added advantage of holding moisture and thus is useful in sandy soils. Both of these materials are expensive if used in large quantities.

The organic gardener uses these inorganic materials from time to time. However, the first goal is always to increase the organic content and life-world in the soil; that will amend the structure and do other good things as well.

NITROGEN, PHOSPHORUS, AND POTASH

The famous triumvirate NPK—nitrogen, phosphorus, and potash—is essential to plant growth. These chemical elements can be supplied in the form of chemical fertilizers, but the organic gardener prefers to use natural sources. Some chemical fertilizers contain harmful by-products, and even the best of them are transformed and then released for plant food only by the action of soil bacteria and fungi. We feel that the living organisms in the soil should be thought of first. They do the work there, and organic material is their normal fare.

Of the NPK group we will consider only nitrogen at this point. An examination of its activities will show the complexity of soil life. Nitrogen is found both in the soil and in the air. Nitrogen also comes from the decay of organic matter in the soil, though it takes more than one kind of organism and more than one step to transform it into the kind plants can use for food. Various soil workers change material from nitrite to nitrate nitrogen, the latter being usable plant food. Unfortunately, the organisms involved in the final step are extremely sensitive to chemicals and to highly acid conditions. Among the destructive chemicals are poison sprays that destroy parts of the soil life-world. Soil scientists have demonstrated that there are from three to fifty times as many soil organisms in the root zone of a plant as away from it. Pretty obviously, the two life-worlds, that of the green plants above and that of minute plants and animals in the soil, have a need for each other.

By now it should be clear that soil is a complex material. The ancient Greeks divided the whole physical world into four "elements": Earth, Air, Fire, and Water. But soil is certainly more than Earth; it is obviously Air and Water too, and less obviously it is Fire in many forms—the heat of the sun, volcanic activity, even the slow oxidation of decay. Like so much of nature, soil is a subtle combination of elements—and it is the aim of the organic gardener to work with this combination rather than against it.

Opposite
A completely natural soil gives birth to this lush vegetation in Miss Tilly's poison-free garden. *Richard F. Conrat photo*

3. Composting and Mulching

Any area of the garden that has a higher-than-average humus content produces healthier plants. Even the non-gardener will note the difference. In addition to its richness, humus-laden soil is valuable because it holds moisture better—taking in more water without runoff and drying out less quickly.

We are familiar with the humus that builds up on forest floors, particularly where there are many deciduous trees. It is called leaf-mold, but is actually the combined product of many natural materials, not only leaves but limbs and trunks rotting. Mushrooms rise and fall, sending the threads that support them through leaves and rotting wood alike. The dung of all the small and large animals that inhabit the forest and the unseen work of earthworms and microbes is added to this rich soil.

Humus is a consumable material. It is used up by the trees and plants, it provides food for necessary soil life, and some of it is always being washed or blown away. So, even under the best of circumstances, humus has to be replaced.

Home gardeners practice the most intensive "farming" known. They expect crops in all four seasons, if possible, one on top of the other in the same soil. There is never a chance to let part of the garden lie fallow or to plant a section with alfalfa. What they demand is a massed array of flowers, vegetables, trees, and shrubs, and probably many things growing more closely together than any farmer would think wise. All this burns up the humus already in the soil.

Since humus is so desirable, can't we make it in quantity and add it to the garden soil? We can, indeed. The method is called "composting."

MATERIALS FOR THE COMPOST HEAP

For the sake of speed and convenience, garden compost production is confined to a heap or bin. It requires only the surplus green matter from the garden—or leaves raked off lawns and walks—a little soil, and some animal manure. If manure is not available there are a number of substitutes which work equally well, and they may be preferred by the fastidious. Trimmings, cuttings, lawn clippings, and the like are laid down in a layer six inches deep. There is no need to measure, as some things are springy and others compactable, so try to mix them when you can.

On top of this layer of green clippings, add a thin layer of manure or some substitute. The purpose of this is to provide extra nitrogen to feed the bacteria and fungi which break down the organic material. Over each layer, add a thin cover of soil to hold in the increasing heat. If it is spring, and you are including the sod of roots, the soil clinging to these will be enough. On each layer some lime should be sprinkled.

The size of the compost heap will depend on how fast new layers can be added, because you don't want the fermenting bottom layer to go cold before the next is added. If it does, your compost will be a long time in the making. The smallest

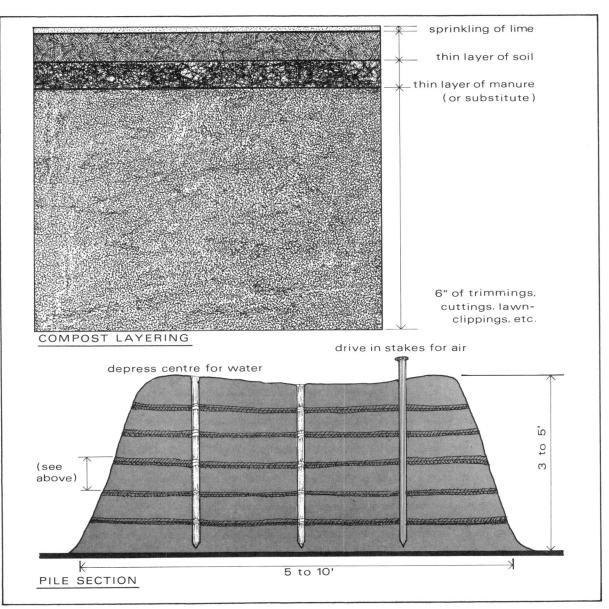

sprinkling of lime

thin layer of soil

thin layer of manure
(or substitute)

6" of trimmings,
cuttings, lawn-
clippings, etc.

COMPOST LAYERING

drive in stakes for air

depress centre for water

3 to 5'

(see
above)

5 to 10'

PILE SECTION

Compost pile. *Drawing by Adrián Martínez*

23

A compost heap in the making. The layer of weeds has been topped with wood ashes and cottonseed meal. A thin layer of soil will be added next.
Joyce R. Wilson photo

workable size would be a 4-by-5-foot wooden bin, a good start for a small garden or city lot. Material shrinks down rapidly when the various processes start. The width of an open pit can be anywhere between five to ten feet at the bottom, with slides sloping up to a flat top, like an Aztec pyramid. The length of the pile doesn't matter, but you will want to get it shaped up and heating as rapidly as possible, so don't extend it beyond your materials.

It is never difficult to get enough garden trimmings and kitchen waste for the start of at least a small compost pile. Getting and adding manure may be a greater problem. What is needed is actually nitrogen, which bacteria and fungi consume in transforming the "trash" into rich, crumbly compost. Without this extra nitrogen, the pile may stand for a whole year and still not be completely decomposed; you need at least a 2 percent nitrogen additive. Chemical nitrogens are not acceptable, as they destroy the soil microorganisms that do the work.

Pulverized and sterilized steer manure of exactly 2 percent nitrogen can be purchased in tidy plastic sacks. There is almost no odor to manure in this form once the layer of dirt has been put over it. However, if you live in close quarters and someone objects, there are perfectly good substitutes. Cottonseed meal is my favorite. It contains 6 percent nitrogen and is easy to sprinkle over the pile.

Two standard sources of nitrogen, both 13 percent, are bloodmeal, and hoof and hornmeal. These are only for distantly placed compost heaps, since the latter may attract flies, and the former has an unpleasant smell for a few days even when covered. Treated sewage sludge sounds bad but is actually easy to handle and pleasantly earthy in odor. Bone meal is also good and will have the additional benefit of correcting acidity and adding phosphates and potash.

A dressing of compost for a vegetable garden. This pile contains a high percentage of redwood sawdust, now well rotted. *Joyce R. Wilson photo*

Fertilizer Values of Some Common Organic Substances

	Nitrogen %	Phosphorus %	Potassium %
Hoof and horn meal	13		
Blood meal	13		
Fish meals	9–14	3 or more	
Bone meal[1]	3	12–24	
Cottonseed meal[1]	7	1.1	1.36
Castor pomace	6		
Buckwheat middlings	4.75	1	1
Meat and bone scraps	8	5	
Sunflower seed oil cake	5.5	1	1
Dry steer and cow manure[2]	2		
Wood ashes			2.5–5
Alfalfa hay[3]	2.35	.21	2

[1] The combination of bone meal, a base high in phosphorus, with cottonseed meal—on the acid side but rich in nitrogen—makes up a gardener's best supplemental fertilizer.

[2] When farmyard manures are used in large quantities, the potassium content of the soil will be maintained, even though the percentage of it in manures is small.

[3] Spoiled alfalfa hay loses some of its nitrogen in the process of bacterial spoilage, but it is still ideal for compost heap or mulch.

ACTIVATING THE COMPOST HEAP

Are activators or starters necessary to get a compost heap under way? Essentially they are not. There will be plenty of bacteria on the material you are composting, and all that is needed is the extra nitrogen supply to get them into intense activity.

On the other hand, I think it is a good practice to include some of the composted material from another heap, because it will certainly contain a splendid cross-culture of the microorganisms that will go to work for you. Even this addition is not necessary, but it seems to set things going rapidly.

There are other activators on the market, one being a liquid in which compost has been soaked— comparable to strong solutions of manure water, but made from compost. The second type of activator is herbal in nature. It is called the ''quick return'' system of composting, and its speed is supposed to be due to the herbs in the activator. You can buy this ''secret formula'' activator from Nichols Garden Nursery in Oregon.

The formula for these activators runs something like: yarrow, dead nettle, chamomile, and honey. These are dried and pulverized, and then the powder is made into a dilute solution which can be added to the beginning compost pile. The sugar in honey, the most rapidly decomposed of all organic substances, may start things immediately— it is gone in hours. Then, too, different plants have individual chemical make-ups and different bacteria attack them in the process of decay. Although such formulas have value in some cases, don't hold up the start of your composting waiting for them. After you have several piles, speed will not be a factor, and it is controlled by weather, season, and other influences.

AIR AND HEAT

Some air will be needed inside the compost pile. There are organisms that work only in the presence of air and others that don't require it, but in the method of composting that we are following, air is as necessary as moisture. To provide it, many people drive stakes into the pile and then remove them when it is finished, thus leaving air tubes to the bottom. Another means of providing ventilation is to put a few coarse limbs or even poles at the bottom of the heap, cross-hatching them to form a base.

Moisture is imperative. Often it will be supplied by the green stuffs of the pile, but there are times of the year and types of contents that may make sprinkling necessary. If there are dry leaves, dry grass, or straw, these will have to be sprinkled well—not soaked, however, as that would exclude the air from your heap. For the same reason, it may be necessary to put some kind of roof or drain over the pile when rains are heavy and prolonged. A waterlogged pile will not heat and it tends to putrefy rather than decay.

Rapid decomposition gives off heat, which seems to encourage further decomposition. If a pile is too small, heat doesn't build up, so we try to make as much of a pile at one time as we can. Since composting is a layering process, this is not too difficult. A couple of layers that have warmed up will be underneath succeeding levels of the pile. If you are not too tardy with additions, each succeeding layer will be warmed by those below it.

Heat has a valuable side effect in addition to its role in rapid decomposition. Prolonged moderate heat kills many organisms, as we know from pasteurizing milk. Weed seeds are also destroyed. Some viruses will be killed at a temperature

of about 160 degrees, so it will be seen that a hot decomposition has values over simply spreading mulches on the ground where they will decay coolly.

CHOPPING AND TURNING

Chopping up material destined for the compost heap has a bearing on temperature. Coarse materials decay slowly and hence coolly. The microbes that break down this material can feed mainly on broken surfaces. The more broken cells there are, the faster they go to work. If you chop, grind, or shred the compost material, it is easy to see that there will be vastly more broken surfaces. Chopping also has a second advantage: it makes turning the heap a very simple task.

For chopping, some people use an ordinary 18-inch rotary lawnmower, which works fairly well on light materials. There is also a make-it-yourself chopper which can be attached to a mower. There are light, inexpensive hoppers with rotary blades in the bottom, but if you want to shred material tougher than leaves, something heavier will be needed. The hammermill types come in several sizes, up to those which will shred three-quarter-inch limbs. While more expensive, they will take care of all your trash problems as well as providing a great bulk of material for mulching. (See Appendix for description of machines and dealers.)

Turning the compost heap at least once is useful, but there is an alternative for those not able to do this. The reason for turning is that the heat in the center of the pile will have killed weed seeds, runners of unwanted plants, and the like, but the outside layer will not have gotten this benefit. Thus the outside layer should be mixed back into the center of the pile after a few days. Some people even give the pile a second turning after a week or so, and if the material has been shredded, this is no great chore.

The alternative for the non-chopper is to keep more than one compost heap going. When you determine that the bulk interior is ripe—this takes about three months on the average—start another pile. For this one, you can fork off the outside layer of the old pile and put it in the center of the new one, where it will make a good heart when mixed with fresh green matter.

THE COMPOST BIN

For pure good looks, it's hard to beat several natural compost piles around a vegetable garden—one pile in the building-up stage, one ready to use as each row is planted, and one in the ripening process. But on a small city lot, bins may be more in tune with the setting; also if you have only a small amount of material to compost, a 4-by-5-foot box will serve better than an open pile. The bin will prevent too-rapid drying out in hot weather, and it will contain the heat better in cold weather.

Bins can be made of 2-by-12-inch planks set inside posts and fixed on three sides. The fourth side should be removable for access. Redwood and cypress are preferred since they resist decay, but the bacteria that make the compost will decompose any wood in time. For this reason, concrete blocks may be best. There is no need to mortar them together, as side pressure is slight, and if they are free, you can remove or add a few to make the bin fit the material of the moment.

Any kind of bin will tend to catch and hold more rainwater than an open heap with sloping sides, so some kind of cover will be necessary for periods of heavy rain. A few sheets of fiberglass will do very well, or the very inexpensive black polyethylene plastic. In either case, have a 4-inch-square timber handy to put on one wall to give some slope and drainage to the cover.

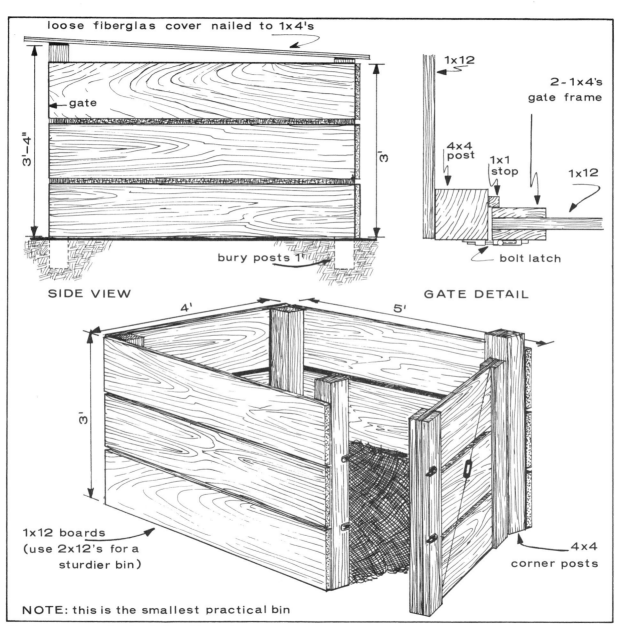

loose fiberglas cover nailed to 1x4's

gate

3'-4"

3'

bury posts 1'

SIDE VIEW

1x12

4x4 post

1x1 stop

2-1x4's gate frame

1x12

bolt latch

GATE DETAIL

4'

5'

3'

1x12 boards (use 2x12's for a sturdier bin)

4x4 corner posts

NOTE: this is the smallest practical bin

Wood compost bin. *Drawing by Don Giannoni*

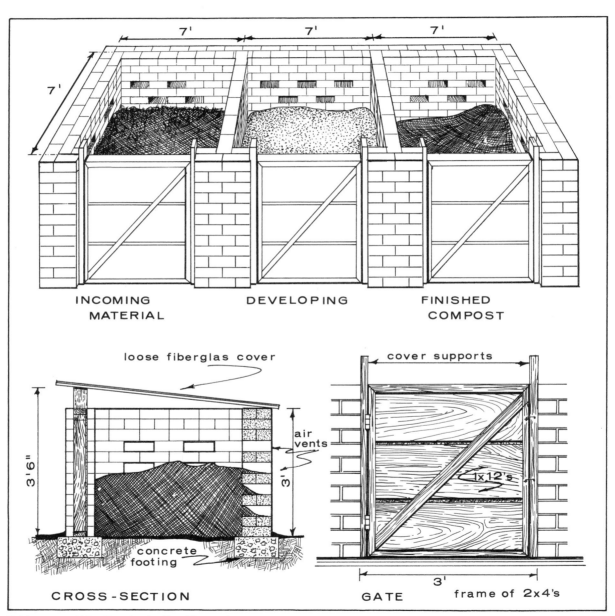

7'   7'   7'

7'

INCOMING
MATERIAL

DEVELOPING

FINISHED
COMPOST

loose fiberglas cover

cover supports

air
vents

3'6"

3'

1x12's

concrete
footing

CROSS-SECTION

GATE   frame of 2x4's

3'

Brick compost bin. *Drawing by Don Giannoni*

EXTRA GRIST

The organic gardener wants a living soil—one rich enough to feed his plants and provide resistance to plant diseases, and to absorb and retain moisture. In short, the gardener needs compost throughout the garden, not just here and there.

To create a living soil, you will need an organic content of between 3 percent and 5 percent in the top six inches of all your garden soil. That content is easily reached, though not if the only composted material consists of lawn clippings and autumn leaves. Once your eye has taken in everything compostable on home grounds, you will begin to think about outside sources.

Sawdust can usually be obtained free from planing mills or sawmills, particularly now that there are more restrictions on burning. Sawdust is very slow to decay, but easy to handle. You can keep a pile on hand and sprinkle a few shovelfuls on each layer of the compost heap. If you buy sawdust, be sure to check for additives. Much sawdust is "rectified" by the addition of some chemical source of nitrogen, such as ammonium sulfate. In any quantity, these chemicals are fatal to earthworms and other soil organisms.

Spoiled hay is a first-rate source of compost material, particularly if it is nitrogen-rich alfalfa or clover. Even the city dweller can get this hay cheaply if he follows the classified ads under farm sections. Feed stores in the horse suburbs often have a few bales kicked aside or returned because of mold, and you can get these for little or nothing.

There are also untidy materials of great value that can be used if you live in the country and have a little space. Pomace—the residue left after pressing of fruits—from wineries or from tomato-juice canneries is excellent; seaweed or kelp is also worth gathering, if it is available. In fact, all fruit and vegetable processing plants have usable wastes.

LIME AND THE pH MEASURE

Any compost pile left to itself will produce an acid humus. This is so because most, but not all, leaves are acid, as are other green stuffs and manure. The processes of decay also produce humic acids.

Some plants prefer an acid soil—notably azaleas, camellias, rhododendrons, and fuchsias. For these you may let the pile alone and use an acid humus. However, most common flowers and vegetables like a slightly acid to neutral soil. To provide that, sprinkle a little ground limestone over each layer of the building pile to correct acidity. Guesswork may succeed, but it is always better to know what you are doing, so simple tests are worthwhile.

Acidity and alkalinity are measured on a pH scale from one to fourteen. One on the scale is strongly acid; seven is neutral; ten or above is very alkaline. Potatoes will grow in a very acid soil, and turnips in one that is very alkaline, yet even these plants tend to prefer the middle. So we aim for a soil that is slightly acid or neutral, between about 5.5 and 7.

In short, you can lime a compost pit heavily with no harm, but it is better to know what you are doing, and that involves testing. Two tests are necessary: one of the compost and another of the soil to which it will be applied. In a general way, it can be said that soils in the eastern United States are acid, while soils in the arid sections of the West tend to the alkaline. However, it is your own garden plot or field that you need to know, so that you can avoid adding an acid compost to a soil already acid, or the other way around.

The test is a very simple matter. You can buy a test tape which looks like a spring-type measuring tape and contains litmus paper, which reacts to acids and bases. The cost is only $1.50. The tapes are available by mail from Park Seed Co. and other suppliers. The soil or the finished compost to be tested is dissolved in a little water in a phial. When the test paper is dipped into this, it will turn a different color depending on the degree of acidity. (If you have a regular soil-test kit, the sample is placed in a reagent rather than water.) There is a color card included with which to match the test paper. A pH of 4—very acid—will turn the paper yellow. If the pH is 8, or extremely alkaline, the paper will turn purple. The slightly acid to neutral sample will be blue-green, and that is generally what one wants.

LIME AND ASHES

More than one sort of material is called limestone. The gardener should know that the kind needed for the compost heap is ground-up sedimentary rock—chemically, calcium carbonate. It may also contain carbonate of magnesium, in the variety called dolomite lime. The latter is an important trace element of value to plants. If the price is right, by all means get it. What you don't want for the compost heap are treated limestones. Pulverized limestone is heated to about a thousand degrees in a lime kiln, and transformed into lye or calcium oxide. Obviously, you wouldn't use that because it would burn and kill all microorganisms.

Nor should you use slack lime (which is readily available), as it is too caustic for the compost pile and will kill earthworms and other organisms. If you can't find pure, simple, ground limestone, it will be better to buy some other base, such as ground bone meal. Though expensive, this supplies additional fertilizing elements in an organic form— that is, slow-acting, derived from living matter, and natural to normal soil processes.

There are other sources of natural lime that come from the sea; ground oyster shells are a good source.

THE USE OF COMPOST

Once you have the rich, crumbly, black, ripe compost, the question is how to make the most of a modest supply. First of all, don't bury it. Put it on top and hoe it in lightly so that the life processes in the surface soil will continue. Feeder roots from tender plants can easily reach it there and draw out their nutrients. A forest floor, which we are trying to imitate, has its organic matter on or near the surface.

If you have only a small amount of ripe compost, a liquid fertilizer may be the optimum use. Liquid fertilizer made from compost is unsurpassed for feeding houseplants in winter or for encouraging tender seedlings in flats. It is the mildest fertilizer possible, yet it contains everything that a plant needs.

In the old days, liquid manures were made in barrels. A plastic garbage can works even better. Fill one of these about a quarter full with the ripe compost; then fill the plastic can with water, rainwater if you can get it. For several days thereafter, stir the contents together. The result will be a dark brew.

If you have quite a bit of compost but not enough to do all the things you would like, the compost can be stretched in combination with mulches. Spread a thin layer of compost, then cover it with a mulch of straw, lawn clippings, or sawdust. The microbes will go to work again, though slowly. What you have is another compost heap, but one spread out flat like a map. Keep in mind that it, too, will need extra nitrogen, so add cottonseed meal or something similar that will replace the nitrogen used up in the process of decay.

DISADVANTAGES OF "GREEN MANURING"

Labor is what most people are concerned about when they think of "green manuring"—that is, planting cover crops and then spading or tilling them under at planting time. There is much good in this procedure if it is done wisely and, in the long run, it is all good. But recent University of California studies have shown that it may take years or even decades for the nutrients to make a complete cycle and come back to the plants you want to grow.

In simple terms, nitrogen will be used up in the process of decay, thus robbing your plants rather than feeding them. By the time this one fertilizing agent is released, your flowers will have bloomed and departed long since. This fact is well known, and all too many gardeners add a nitrate-producing chemical to the soil as a compensating factor. The effect of such a chemical drench is to halt or destroy the activity of soil microorganisms.

When spading under green manure, remember to use only organic sources of nitrogen: animal manure, cottonseed meal, fish meal, and the like. These will become a part of the cycle rather than inhibiting it. Still, to provide a living heart to the soil, nothing compares with compost. Everything in the rich black humus is ready. The violent stage of breakdown and decay is over. All the elements are ready to become healthy, living plants again.

Opposite
Keep on hand a supply of various organics. Those pictured include cow manure, cottonseed meal, compost, and well-rotted sawdust. *Joyce R. Wilson photo*

4. Earthworms and Humus

Earthworms are very primitive animals that have barely made their way out of the water in the evolutionary scale. They like moist places rich in humus or decayed organic matter. Curiously enough, these children of the water have been of vast importance in building up the living land—they have been part of the process for eighty million years or more. Erosion and climatic changes will break up basic rock, but it takes the earthworm to grind up in its gizzard both minerals and organic matter. This valuable combination of ingredients is then extruded as castings, and a living soil is under way.

Charles Darwin spent forty years studying earthworms and their habits. He actually weighed castings on measured plots and found 14 to 18 tons of castings per acre on English soil. His figures have been confirmed by modern research. It has also been shown that in deltas, such as that of the Nile in Egypt, earthworms may produce up to 120 tons of castings per acre in a single year.

Earthworms could be considered the mammoths of the life-world in the soil. Some from Ecuador and Australia grow to be an inch in diameter and seven feet long, yet even small worms are giants when compared to the various other organisms, such as microbes, that work in the soil. The functions of all of them are broadly similar—that of breaking down and transforming formerly living matter so that it will be available for food for plants about to grow again. It is a matter of transforming the past into the future.

Undoubtedly, we do want to take advantage of these natural helpers, but limitations and means must be considered. First of all, one should keep in mind that earthworms do not create richness from nothing, out of the void. Earthworms are simply transformers or soil brokers. They can't live on minerals or chemical elements alone, and many chemicals will kill them outright.

The energy they generate to do their work comes from organic matter, whether fresh or otherwise. They thrive on manure, decaying matter, fallen leaves, or grease from the kitchen. If you supply the earthworms with this source of food they will do the digging, the grinding, the combining, and then return a soil that is rich and loose. Water will penetrate it, and air will follow down the same passages. Fertilizer formed in the process (and there can be tons of castings) is mild. It is a cool fertilizer that will not harm any plants, no matter how tender.

There is no point in growing earthworms and then planting them in a dense clay soil. They can't live there, so they will leave or die. To do their work, they must have organic food, which can be either ripe compost or raw organic matter. The kinds of earthworms that you can buy and raise do very well on raw wastes and kitchen refuse.

NATIVE WORMS

Native worms—hardly a scientific category but a handy way of thinking about earthworms— are already in your soil. These are the kinds you don't have to buy. Native worms in the East are not

Earthworms released into soil to improve the productivity of the earth. *USDA photo*

the same as those in the West, but they have one quality in common. Both are slow to reproduce. (By contrast, the red worms, which are the kind you buy, reproduce very rapidly.) However, when well fed, native worms increase greatly. In time, there will be as many of these worms in your garden soil as there is food available, supplied by compost and mulches. In addition to tilling the soil, the worms contain 1½ to 2 percent nitrogen in their bodies. The Connecticut Experiment Station ran tests which showed that the castings contained four to five times as much nitrate nitrogen as did identical soil which was wormless. The increase in phosphate and potassium in castings over wormless soil was even greater.

Undoubtedly, it is best to encourage these natives. It takes less effort than raising worms artificially, and these worms will dig down deeply, whereas the red and manure worms are surface feeders. Deeper burrowing brings up valuable minerals and, in time, works these into the topsoil. The natives are also more tolerant of variations in temperature and moisture. If the topsoil gets too hot or cold, or too dry, they can just dig in deeper.

MANURE WORMS AND RED WORMS

Red worms, perhaps with some fancy addition to the name, are the ones you will probably buy to raise in boxes or pits. They have to be kept moist at all times, and in cold climates need some shelter. Under the right conditions, a breeding red worm will produce an egg capsule every week or ten days. These capsules are multiple, so that from two to twenty worms hatch from each one. Each of these new worms will come to breeding age in two to three months. Since worms are bisexual (even though they have to mate to bear), all of the increase will be breeders.

The gardener can use these worms in a number of ways. One way is to introduce red worms into the compost heap as soon as it cools. There they will quickly set to work grinding up the organic material. When planting them in the heap, don't scatter them around, but put them in a single clump. They like to know where their fellows are before they set off in cautious exploration.

Earthworms are as conservative as cats about changing their environment or leaving home. When possible, it is a good idea to plant the egg capsules in the new medium, or include some of the original material when transplanting. If the worms were raised in a box of half peat and half horse manure, include a good portion of that when setting them out in the compost.

If there is a continuing supply of manure on the premises, from chickens, rabbits, cows, horses, or other animals, red worms will break down the manure so that you can use it without fear of burning plants. If the manure has been piled, it will heat up—so wait for cooling. Better yet, spread it out in a layer a foot deep, perhaps mixing in some soil, and it will not heat. Some ground limestone should be sprinkled on straight manure. Earthworms have a calcium-secreting gland near the gizzard which allows them to digest this highly acid material, but they cannot live in a highly acid soil—hence the need for litter, soil, or the like to which they can retreat after feeding.

To be sure red worms really work for you, feed kitchen refuse and vegetable garden discards directly into their beds, whether these are boxes, tubs, or more elaborate pits. This makes a sort of running compost heap or living garbage can, which can be transformed daily as you add the lighter trimmings.

Red worms will also thrive in the top foot or so of your garden soil, if it is rich and moist and given an occasional supplemental feeding. This works best if you are also mulching the soil with grass clippings, chopped straw, or similar material. Such mulches keep the ground cool and moist and will be eaten in time by the worms. For a supplement, a little chicken mash or other concentrate can be sprinkled on top of the soil where the worms will soon find it.

If manure worms or red worms are going to be used in any of these ways, they will have to be propagated. The egg capsules and young worms should be gathered and planted where you want them. The procedure can be compared to starting a sour-dough yeast and using a bit to make bread. People who grow these worms for fish bait use a mixture of half peat moss—to retain moisture—and half manure.

For breeding earthworms, a lug box, tub, or or even a five-gallon bucket will do. Drainage is important because these worms do not breed in a soggy bed. They thrive best when the temperature of their surroundings is between 60 and 80 degrees, but will survive without multiplying at lower temperatures. The manure mixed in with the soil and peat or straw will usually be plenty of food for the worms. If you do add cottonseed meal, chicken mash, or other concentrates, be very sparing. Sprinkle only a little on top of the soil. Like other animals, worms can have too much food and will suffer from excess protein.

My red worms live in lug boxes with a soil and manure mix about six inches deep. Every month or so I turn out the contents and divide the egg capsules and the immature worms. The breeders can be recognized by a thickened white band around their middles. Some of the soil and castings are put in the potting-soil pile; fresh manure and soil are added to the box. These boxes are kept under a bench in a shed which serves as a semi-greenhouse, since it has fiberglass sides and stays above freezing inside. The increase can be planted in another box added to the compost pile, or planted directly in the vegetable garden.

All this depends on the season and the need.

The encouragement of earthworms, by whatever methods you want to use, is a basic principle of good soil management. Combined with composting and the encouragement of other soil organisms, earthworms will help produce the kind of living soil needed for a healthy garden—a garden that by its very nature will have a balance of nature, so that poisonous sprays and herbicides will not be necessary. Good soil helps to produce healthy plants, and healthy plants are seldom attacked by insects.

Unseen earthworms are at work for you. There were none in the pot at the left; the middle pot contains only dead worms; the pot on the right contains living, working worms. *USDA photo*

41

5. Birds

Birds are the most effective and persistent insecticides that have ever existed. They reach the undersides of leaves and other places that sprays miss. Furthermore, they cost the gardener nothing—unless he counts the small amount of fruits they may eat.

ATTRACTING BIRDS

Since most common garden birds are insect-eaters, we should try to attract and keep them around our house and grounds. A very few of the common garden birds eat some fruit and berries in addition to their basic diet of insects. In these cases, we want to get their benefits and, at the same time, prevent the damage they may do in season. But preventing occasional damage from birds is simple compared to the problem of checking the work of chewing, sucking, and blighting insects.

There are very few birds which cannot be encouraged to stay in the garden, if the gardener carefully observes their habits and wants. Bluebirds are the harbingers of spring in many places, and their appearance might seem a chance blessing. These birds, which have the blue of the sky on their backs and the brown of the earth underneath, prefer caterpillars as food. They also like grasshoppers and other insects, and they injure nothing at all.

Eastern bluebirds are very hardy spirits and dare the cold to return early in the spring. If late blizzards overtake them, they find protection in hollows of any kind, so it is good to provide the bluebirds and others a refuge in the garden or nearby. Since natural cavities in old trees are the most attractive, think carefully before cementing them up. It may be possible to seal only the bottom of a hole to protect the tree from further rot, and thereby preserve a nesting refuge for any number of garden birds.

Swallows are birds that form a kind of protective roof over the garden. A few feet above us, they sweep the sky for nocturnal bugs. Their throats are larger than those of other birds, and their open mouths, like nets, trap animal life in the air. Barn swallows will gladly move into the eaves of outbuildings, from which they can sally forth for invaluable hunting.

The swallow that is the greatest friend to man is the purple martin. In remote times, it probably nested in hollow trees as bluebirds do, but long ago the American Indian discovered the value of these birds in controlling village insects. The Indians hung gourds with openings about their

Opposite
Barn swallows do nothing but good. They sweep the air over the garden, cleaning it of insects. *USDA photo*

42

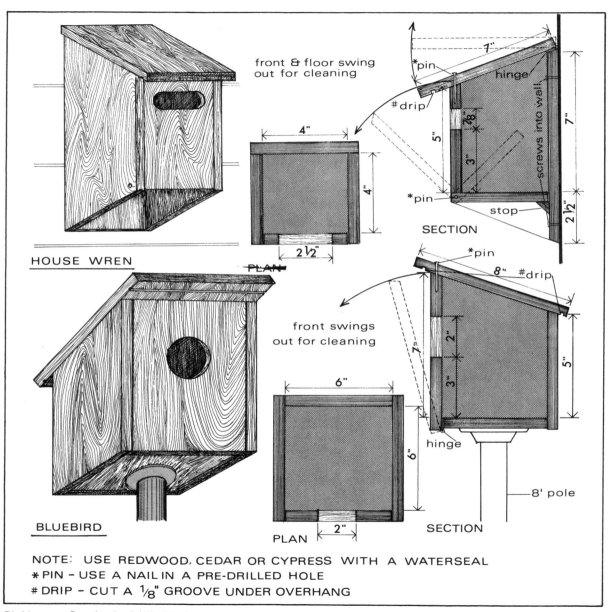

front & floor swing
out for cleaning

*pin

#drip

hinge

screws into wall

7"

7"

5"

3"

7/8"

*pin

stop

2½"

SECTION

4"

4"

2½"

HOUSE WREN   PLAN

BLUEBIRD

front swings
out for cleaning

*pin   #drip

8"

2"

5"

7"

3"

hinge

8' pole

SECTION

6"

6"

2"

PLAN

NOTE: USE REDWOOD, CEDAR OR CYPRESS WITH A WATERSEAL
* PIN – USE A NAIL IN A PRE-DRILLED HOLE
# DRIP – CUT A ⅛" GROOVE UNDER OVERHANG

44   Bird houses. *Drawing by Adrián Martínez*

camp for the martins to use. Apparently, the birds liked this kind of companionship, for they now choose bird houses in preference to natural places. Thirty or more martins will nest in a community house, feeding on flies, wasps, true bugs, and other unwanted summer visitors.

Once winter has passed, the gardener looks for the brilliant black and orange oriole. In the East it is the Baltimore oriole, while the West has a counterpart and look-alike, the Bullock oriole. The basic food for both consists of caterpillars, pupae, and adult moths. Once the oriole young have hatched, both parents begin the work of bringing food to them. I have watched male and female alternately bringing in large tent caterpillars at about one-minute intervals. My good luck orioles also like small insects such as black-olive scale.

Another group of birds that catch many insects on the wing is the flycatcher family, of which the kingbird is a familiar example. My favorite in the group is the black phoebe; he is a year-round resident here, and his constant aid in catching insects is priceless. Flycatchers don't get all their food on the wing, though; they also pick caterpillars and eat countless aphids.

There are some birds, not truly domestic, that nevertheless do the garden great good while they stay. Some kinds of warblers are quite secretive and may be heard rather than seen. Where I live, the only friendly species is the Audubon's warbler.

While only a small number of birds are drawn to artificial bird houses, all birds are attracted to water. Especially in the Far West, where there may be little rain from May to October, water will draw birds from great distances. The observant gardener knows that birds differ in their bathing and drinking habits. Some birds like to flutter in the shallows of a conventional birdbath. Others, like the brown towhee, are thoroughgoing baptists who insist on complete submersion. At the opposite extreme

is the shy bluebird who will not wet its feet, but loves a fine mist.

Since many plants prefer a fine mist to a drenching shower, it is doubly useful to provide a spot or two in the garden with a fixed pipe, a few feet about ground level, with a fine nozzle. All kinds of birds will fly through this. None will be more beautiful than a family of bluebirds taking turns, dipping through the rainbow and mist once or twice, then setting on a nearby limb to dry and preen themselves.

If you wish to attract birds to the garden, you must remember to vary the water supply. Don't depend upon one Grecian pedestal of possibly stagnant water in a basin. Birds, like people, have certain favorite times of day for bathing and drinking. Doves, for instance, take all their water at sundown. Therefore, the gardener who wants to attract more birds than his neighbor will have some water available at all hours, and in a number of forms—in pools, in sprays, and if possible, flowing.

The gardener will think, too, of encouraging helpful birds by providing some food during the cold weather.

A good method for winter feeding of those birds that don't like to eat on the ground is to hang feeders in trees or from eaves. You can buy automatic seed hoppers or make them at home. Drill ¾-inch holes into a length of 2-inch-square wood; then mix bacon fat or lard with seed and fill the holes. Hang this feeder by a wire, and perhaps add a perch. Many varieties of birds are attracted to this rich combination of fat and seed.

SOME SMALL FRIENDLY BIRDS

While the birds mentioned so far are somewhat shy in the immediate presence of man, there are some small insect-eaters that are very friendly to the gardener. The foremost of these are the wrens.

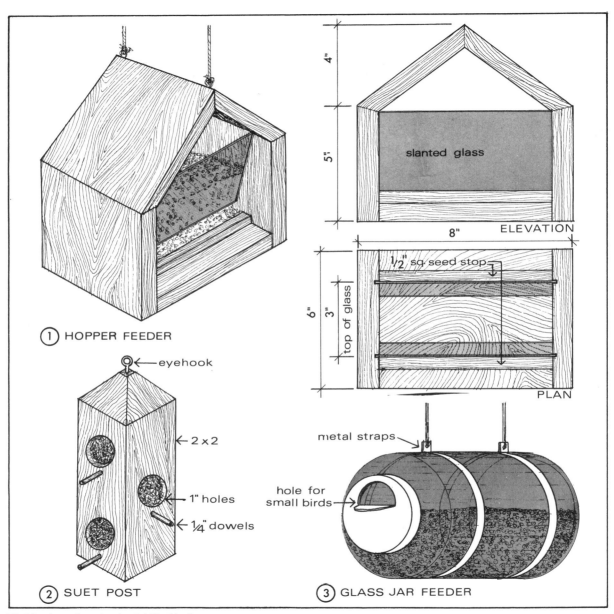

① HOPPER FEEDER

4"

5"

slanted glass

8" ELEVATION

½" sq seed stop

6"

3"

top of glass

PLAN

eyehook

← 2 x 2

1" holes

¼" dowels

② SUET POST

metal straps

hole for
small birds

③ GLASS JAR FEEDER

Bird feeders. *Drawing by Adrián Martínez*

One day I went into my small greenhouse and found a Bewick wren making a pot-by-pot inspection. While I stood within a foot or two, the tiny wren inspected each stem and leaf. From time to time it discovered and devoured some minute insect or egg. After perhaps an hour of this diligent work, it hopped down from the bench to strut out into the garden.

Wrens especially like to eat insects belonging to the order Hemiptera, which includes leafhoppers, plant lice, scale insects, whiteflies, and true bugs. Because the wrens are so small, they find it worthwhile to pick up the tiniest of insect eggs. Wrens are cavity-nesters and will take readily to boxes placed in fruit trees where you want the birds to work. Or, if you prefer, you can put a box on the inside wall of a garden shed with a hole bored through the wall for the wren's door. A titmouse will also live in a hole in the wall or in a birdhouse. Its diet is much like that of the wren and all to the gardener's benefit.

In the West and Southwest, there are tiny, dull-looking birds called bushtits. These travel about in flocks and make their way through shrubbery, eating aphids, scale, and the like. Fortunately they are abundant, and a visit from them is like having a hundred wrens pass through the garden. Bushtits are small enough to hang upside down on a leaf while searching it for insects. They move about ceaselessly, never staying long on one tree or shrub. Since they dislike open spaces, they are likely to spend more time where shrubbery is thick.

SOME MOSTLY HELPFUL BIRDS

None of the birds mentioned so far will eat fruits, berries, and vegetables, but there are some otherwise beneficial birds that will. The mockingbird, almost universally liked for its song, eats many grasshoppers, but it also likes grapes and other fruits.

Another large and beautiful bird with an appetite for fruit is the grosbeak: the black-headed grosbeak in the West, the rose-breasted grosbeak in the East. This bird enjoys a diet of more than half insects—beetles being preferred, but caterpillars and even scale insects are included. However, about a quarter of its summer food consists of domestic fruits, especially cherries and figs.

The organic gardener continues to welcome these birds, though they do a small amount of damage. He knows that they do more good than harm, and his garden grows well enough so that he can afford to let birds share a little of its produce. More important, he employs another method to solve the fruit-eating problem: the use of decoy trees and shrubs.

We have a mockingbird that, though a frequent visitor, never bothers fruit because it has a continuous supply of wild or ornamental berries to eat. These seem to be preferred by most birds over the fleshier garden fruits. Elderberries, which grow wild here, are among the earliest fruits to set, and many birds relish them. There is a red-berried variety that is fully ornamental. Our mockingbird moves from elderberries to privet; in the fall, it moves to the Virginia creeper, and the second crop of grapes that has been left to wither.

One of the best decoy trees that can be planted is the white mulberry or silkworm tree. Its fruit, maturing at the same time as cherries, is non-acid, which birds prefer. Other mulberries are also useful in the garden, if placed away from walks so that the falling fruit won't be a bother. Several viburnums have berries relished by birds. The Western robin is happy to dine on pyracantha berries rather than olives, which they occasionally attack. In any case, be sure to have a supply of expendable fruit at all times.

These supplemental food supplies will bring more birds to your garden—and in bad weather,

HOUSE WREN

BLACK PHOEBE

PURPLE MARTIN

PLAIN TITMOUSE

BARN SWALLOW

BROWN TOWHEE

Birds. *Drawings by Charles Hoeppner*

The mockingbird is a fixture in many gardens. Perhaps 10 percent of its diet is grasshoppers, but it will also pilfer fruits and berries. Netting is the best way to keep both fruits and beautiful songs. *USDA photo*

supplements may prevent starvation. In northern California, Oregon, and Washington, we often have winter rains for a month on end. At such times, birds must seek protection from the cold much of the time, and food is scarce, so that they get the least food when they need the most.

Like most members of the sparrow family, the junco or snowbird is primarily a seed-eater, but a quarter of its diet is insects. Since these attractive birds are abundant, they can do much good in winter cleanup. Birdseed scattered on the ground during a storm will bring them to your garden.

A FEW UNDESIRABLE BIRDS

There are very few really undesirable birds in the garden. The English sparrow, which is not a true sparrow, is one of them. Live traps are an effective way of removing these without harming wanted birds. The linnet, or house finch, may be destructive in large numbers; it is responsible for more fruit damage than any other bird.

In the West, the two common jays are undesirable. They eat fruits and nuts and drive away other birds, and they also destroy the nests and eat the eggs of useful birds. Unfortunately, jays are hard to discourage by peaceful means.

Two groups of woodpeckers have a bad reputation, which I think is unjust. Both the hairy and downy woodpeckers occur across the entire country and are everywhere valuable insect eaters. They have the special skill of boring for grubs. While this may look destructive, the grubs are far more damaging. In addition, these birds pick the tree clean of plant lice and scale insects. Sometimes, a woodpecker will drill on a house or barn, in which case you will have to chase it away. There are small explosive devices sold to frighten birds, and you may need to resort to these occasionally.

Blackbirds may seem a sour note to conclude with, but I want to make the point that you should judge birds by what you see, rather than by reputation. They certainly are not all bad. I allowed a flock of Brewer's blackbirds to nest in some conifers one year, just to see what would happen. They ate caterpillars and took grubs and cutworms from newly turned ground. Nevertheless, they still didn't seem to me desirable garden birds, because of their scolding and the dim view they took of the gardener. The next year it was easy to frighten them away from that nesting spot.

When it comes time to rest in the garden, one should sit down and watch some of the garden birds at work. Observation makes for a faster friendship between you and the best pest-destroyers available to any gardener.

HELPFUL AND/OR FRIENDLY BIRDS

There really isn't such a group as "garden birds," even though some are more friendly to man, or like to make use of human surroundings. A great deal depends on where your garden is, whether along a woodsy creek, in town, or in dry upland country. Here in California we often have ruby-crowned kinglets in the garden; in New Mexico, these birds are denizens of the high mountains.

Then there are birds such as owls that may live in or near your garden, yet in spite of the good they do, they are hardly thought of as garden birds. One day I had a peregrine falcon for a half-hour in a top branch, and that was a great thing, but a falcon is not often thought of as a garden bird.

Hence these short lists refer only to the small and useful birds, and then only to a skimming of these. The members of the local Audubon Society will be glad to help in identifying the beneficial birds that frequent your particular garden.

East	South	West	Southwest
hairy woodpecker	ground dove	hairy woodpecker	Lewis' woodpecker
downy woodpecker	whippoorwill	downy woodpecker	Eastern kingbird
Eastern kingbird	downy woodpecker	Western kingbird	Western kingbird
great crested flycatcher	barn swallow	ash-throated flycatcher	black phoebe
Eastern phoebe	tree swallow	black phoebe	Say's phoebe
least flycatcher	tufted titmouse	barn swallow	barn swallow
barn swallow	Carolina chickadee	violet-green swallow	cliff swallow
tree swallow	Carolina wren	plain titmouse	plain titmouse
purple martin	mockingbird	white-breasted nuthatch	house wren
black-capped chickadee	catbird	red-breasted nuthatch	mockingbird
house wren	brown thrasher	Bewick's wren	robin
brown thrasher	robin	mockingbird	Western bluebird
Eastern robin	Eastern bluebird	California thrasher	yellow warbler
wood thrush	myrtle warbler	robin	Bullock's oriole
hermit thrush	Baltimore oriole	hermit thrush	summer tanager
Eastern bluebird	cardinal	Western bluebird	evening grosbeak
Tennessee warbler		loggerhead shrike	lesser goldfinch
Eastern yellow warbler		yellow warbler	brown towhee
Baltimore oriole		Audubon's warbler	
		Bullock's oriole	
		Western tanager	
		black-headed grosbeak	
		lesser (Arkansas) goldfinch	
		rufus-sided towhee	
		brown towhee	
		Oregon junco	
		white-crowned sparrow	

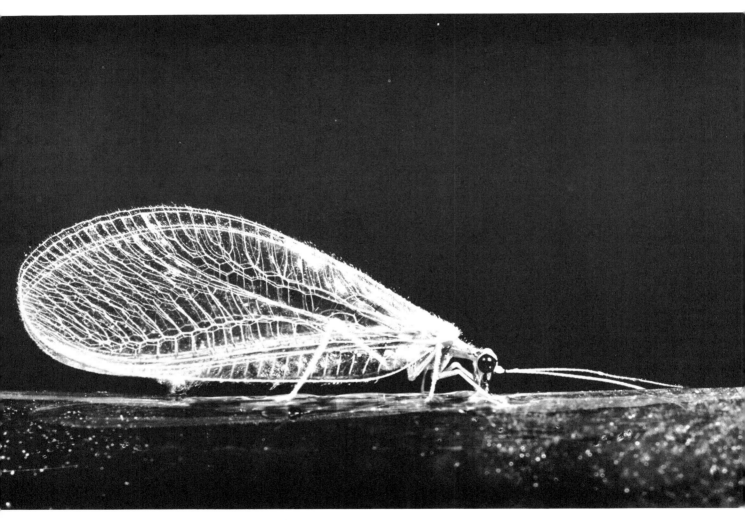

Lacewings are predatory. This one is *Chrysopa oculata.* When you buy
lacewing larvae to spread in garden or field, it is likely to be *Chrysopa
carnea,* but all of the genus look much alike and are equally helpful. Protect
them from poison sprays. *USDA photo*

6. Beneficial Insects

While one is naturally drawn to birds because of their beauty, it is difficult to feel any affection for the vast company of insects. There are too many associations with ruined picnics, so we forget that some insects are valuable, indeed indispensable, to man.

One of their important services is the pollinating of plants. Though some seed-bearing plants are pollinized by the wind, the majority are fertilized by insects. The scattering of pollen from one bloom to another doesn't matter much in the flower garden, but it is significant that most of our fruits and many vegetables are fertilized by insects.

These good deeds scarcely make most gardeners appreciate insects. For one thing, there are so many kinds of insects—some 850,000 of them—though not all are in our gardens, of course. Out of this enormous number, the gardener gets to know well the few large-sized enemies that he sees every year. There are others, minute or scarcely visible, that are familiar only because of the symptoms they produce on plants.

Besides these obvious insect pests there are also mysterious threats: something is getting at your flowers or blighting the vegetables. Because the source of much damage is unknown, insecticide-ad men can make their pitch appealing. You are offered a "broad spectrum" poison. The label very probably lists every pest you have heard of, and then promises more. In one paragraph there are directions for "flying insects." The next tells you how to push the button for "crawling insects." That should just about take care of everything—or so you are led to think.

The use of the "broad spectrum" insecticide is likely to kill all the helpful insects. Many of these you never see; some lay their eggs in grubs or caterpillars and thereby destroy them. Other insects are carnivores rather than parasites and literally stalk and eat your main pests. Some people will argue that we may as well spray with everything and kill all the insects in the garden—without the

53

pests we don't need their enemies either. But it doesn't work out quite that way.

The result may be compared to sneezing in an operating room, where one sneeze would leave a pure culture of unwanted germs. (Though, to be sure, a garden can never be as sterile as an operating room, no matter how much you spray and dust and drench.) All around the garden are myriads waiting to swarm back in; some of these will be old enemies, and some will be new ones ready to exploit a clear field.

I was an unhappy witness to such a regression not long after DDT was introduced. DDT was used to spray the mites that injure prune leaves, and the first year it did quite well. These mites, or red spiders, are not actually insects—they belong with spiders, ticks, and scorpions, though they are infinitesimal. The mites had been kept in check by a tiny true bug *(Triphleps),* which made a specialty of eating the mites. The true bugs were abundant, as were the ladybugs and lacewings that also ate the mites. The sprays killed the lot of them most effectively. Perhaps we should say *a lot* of them rather than *the lot,* for there were red spiders still about, no spray being totally effective.

Then the joker appeared. Red spiders lay eggs when two weeks old and can go through many cycles in one season; the enemies of red spiders were on an annual basis for the most part, or on a slower cycle. It is not hard to guess which insect came back in strength.

At the same time, there were some unexpected effects— like the sneeze in the operating room. New pests turned up that hadn't been a problem or even noticed before. One of my neighbors found that he was spending 10 to 20 percent of his gross income to have more and different sprays applied. Since farmers are apt to be suspicious, he thought that the spray companies may have put something

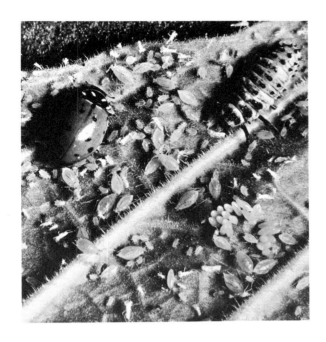

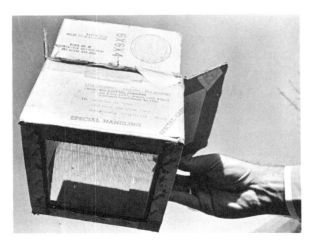

in their concoctions to make new pests. In a sense he was right. He also drew the next conclusion, which was to stop spraying altogether.

That was a wise decision, but the dynamic balance of nature could not return the day or the season he stopped spraying. A sudden change from chemical poisons to an organic approach to the soil and its life-world, and to biological control of pests, may have some difficult moments. In a garden the shift back to reason is easier if a livelihood is not at stake.

There are some immediate measures the farmer or gardener can take to help to right the balance quickly. As soon as drenching with insecticides has stopped, there will be a chance for the microorganisms and the earthworms to begin again. A living soil can hardly be built up in one year, but within three months compost can be applied to the soil.

For insect control, the start can be quicker since there are a growing number of beneficial insects that the farmer or gardener can "plant" on his fields, just as trout are planted in streams and lakes. It is possible to add thousands of insect predators as soon as they are needed in the spring, thus tipping the balance back in favor of the man who tills his soil.

For the gardener of a small plot who would like to avoid poison sprays altogether, there are several predatory or parasitic insects that he can buy and use without any special skill. Not only do they cost less than sprays; they are more effective as well. Usually, sprays are not applied until the pest is obvious—and mature. Much of the damage has then been done, and a new generation of the pest is assured. Sprays never cover all the surfaces, even if a competent man is hired to do the job. One nurseryman told me that 20 to 50 percent was the most he could hope for.

Control of insects *by insects* is another matter. They start early and work thoroughly. Parasites lay their eggs in the eggs of caterpillars. In some cases, these are consumed before the caterpillar even hatches; in others, they are destroyed soon after. For thoroughness, there is nothing like the insect predators. They are busy long before you have noticed that the pests are on your plants. They are hungry to begin with and will patiently search night and day to find their food.

THE LADYBUG

The most familiar predatory insect that you can buy to keep the garden cleaned of pests is the ladybug. (Actually ladybugs are beetles, not bugs, and are more properly called lady*birds*.) Of the many different species in the United States, almost all are highly beneficial. Both the larvae, which look like tiny alligators, and the adult ladybugs feed heavily upon aphids, scale insects, and the eggs and larvae of other small pests. If you have been wise enough not to have used sprays, some of these ladybugs may still be in your garden.

One species, the two-spotted ladybug, will winter over in a house or outbuilding, and in the spring you may see them on the screens trying to get back into your garden. In the West, we have one called the two-stabbed ladybug which specializes in scale insects. Not all kinds are equally easy to use in your garden. Research is being done, and we should have a larger choice before long.

The convergent ladybug is the one most easily obtained. It has the familiar reddish coat and twelve or thirteen black spots on its back. The convergent ladybug will eat forty to fifty aphids a day, and when the supply of these is gone, will turn to scale insects, mealybugs, leafhoppers, or whatever other small pests your garden may have.

A quart jar will hold 18,000 hungry ladybugs, and you can buy that amount, which is enough for a large garden, for a base price of $4.25. A little figuring will show that they could remove a million aphids almost immediately, which is good news if you have apple trees, or if you grow cabbage and sprouts, artichokes, and other hosts to aphids.

There are now professional consultants, called "insect ecologists," available to advise the farmer on what pests he has in what quantity, and how many beneficial insects it would take to check the pests. These consultants work with insectaries and scientists in the production of different kinds of ladybugs to be used against specific pests, such as the mealybug. When insects must be developed in this way rather than simply gathered in, they are more expensive. However, they are still a very good buy, because once control insects establish themselves, there is no additional cost to the gardener or farmer.

Ladybug larvae are not as pretty as the adults, but they are more aggressive. Each one will eat up to 400 insect pests. *USDA photo*

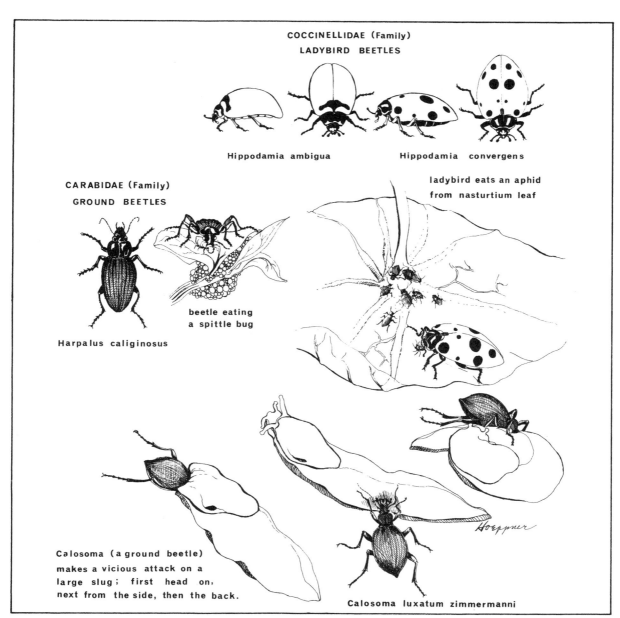

COCCINELLIDAE (Family)
LADYBIRD BEETLES

Hippodamia ambigua   Hippodamia convergens

CARABIDAE (Family)
GROUND BEETLES

ladybird eats an aphid
from nasturtium leaf

beetle eating
a spittle bug

Harpalus caliginosus

Calosoma (a ground beetle)
makes a vicious attack on a
large slug; first head on,
next from the side, then the back.

Calosoma luxatum zimmermanni

Beneficial garden insects. *Drawing by Charles Hoeppner*

THE GREEN LACEWING

A careless gardener might destroy the lacewing when it is discovered crawling up a stem, because it looks as avaricious as a grasshopper. But these insects are no plague, and the long sickle-like jaws are for eating other insects. The lacewing is easily recognized by the delicately patterned, transparent wings for which it is named. Its thread-like antennae, as long as the body, wave about in exploration when the lacewing crawls over plants in search of mites and soft-bodied insects.

In colder sections of the country, only the eggs winter over; but in warmer regions, adult lacewings survive the winter. In either case, there are several broods a year. The larvae mature in a couple of weeks, spin a small cocoon, and after two weeks more, the adults hatch out. Lacewings do eat some ladybug larvae along with the rest of their insect diet, but it is a principle of natural controls that a balance will be maintained. Many useful birds also eat ladybugs and their larvae, which is just one more reason for adding extra predators to the garden.

A few lacewings are particularly useful in a greenhouse or lathhouse, where they will perform a constant patrol in an area where sudden outbursts of pests are more likely than in the open ground. Eggs or small larvae of this predator cost about a penny each in small lots. Once a number of them are established about your place, there is no further cost—and that is very different from having to buy a multitude of sprays each year.

THE PRAYING MANTIS

Mantises are "still hunters." Their sticklike bodies are nearly invisible as they stand and wait for their unsuspecting game. Ladybugs, on the other hand, stalk their prey—like deer hunters. Mantises are not real fliers and they travel at a slow walk, which means that they are very apt to make a permanent home with you rather than drift away to benefit someone else. There are small native species, as well as giant Chinese mantises. The latter, introduced into the Philadelphia area toward the end of the last century, have adapted very well; and because they can survive where the climate is much colder, they have spread northward into areas unfit for native mantises.

Chinese mantises are impressively large, reaching five inches at maturity in late summer. They are *very* hungry carnivores, and insects are their meat. To establish either kind of mantis, buy

Egg case of the Chinese mantis, containing 200 eggs. The case of the native species is much slimmer. In nature, these cases are built around small twigs, but if you buy them they must be suspended in shrubs by threads.
Joyce R. Wilson photo

58

A Chinese mantis emerges mosquito size, but by late summer it may be 5 inches long. At any size, they are helpful carnivores. Native mantises are equally useful but will not survive as much cold weather. *USDA photo*

their egg cases in winter, generally from December on. Each case may contain as many as 200 eggs, which is a happy prospect for any gardener. The cases can simply be hung in a tree or set in the fork of a shrub. Then, by nature's clock, the eggs will hatch when the time is ripe, which is to say when your particular weather has become warm enough to bring out the local insects.

In the greenhouse, a mantis egg case can be placed under a bench, where it will hatch out quickly to take care of any winter pests. If all goes well, the mother mantises will hang new egg cases in your garden the following fall. Like other aspects of nature, mantis populations fluctuate from year to year. Unless you happen to be there when the young hatch out, you may not see any for some time. When first hatched, mantises are tiny mosquito-sized specks, but already extremely hungry. Toward summer, when they have grown to an inch or more, you will see these rather grotesque helpers walking about.

THE WASP

So far we have discussed predatory insects: those that eat other insects. There are also parasites that work more indirectly. One of their methods is to lay their eggs in other insect eggs, so that the hatched parasite consumes the food contained in the larger egg. Sometimes the cycle is slower, and it is not until the host egg has become a caterpillar and is growing that the young parasites attack it for food.

Of the many kinds of parasites, wasps are among the most useful. There are small wasps that are seldom noticed and of no harm to humans. Every year new kinds are being discovered and introduced to combat specific insect pests. Recently, a tiny Mexican wasp (*Amitus spinferus*) was introduced to control the woolly whitefly, a serious citrus pest.

One wasp the gardener can easily buy and use to advantage belongs to the genus *Trichogramma*. One species works on tree caterpillars and another on field crops, the latter making a specialty of the eggs of the alfalfa butterfly. You may not need to control that, but they also parasitize the eggs of other harmful insects, the buffalo leafhopper for one. A quart and a half of these wasps will contain 24,000 individuals ready to go to work. So when you have caterpillar trouble on a large scale, and these pests often do come in repulsive masses, this little wasp is worth a test, especially as the cost is nominal.

THE GROUND BEETLE

There is a group of rather nondescript beetles that any gardener should know. You can't buy them to add to your controls, but you can learn to recognize them and protect them, for they are master carnivores and do almost nothing but good. One kind is said to nibble a strawberry from time to time, but that hasn't been my experience.

The family as a whole are called ground beetles because they are flightless, and many of them are found under stones and logs. One imported member of the family climbs very well in search of prey, and two Eastern members of the family also climb tree trunks in search of insect food. You will meet them most often when a large flower pot or other solid object is moved. Then you will see a number of black or rusty beetles of from a half-inch to an inch long. Being very active, as befits a predaceous character, they will quickly dart away. Don't stamp on them, and don't spray, as they are easily poisoned. If in doubt about identification of these beetles, take one or two to the local biology teacher.

In the West their names are as prosaic as their appearance; there is the "red carabid" or "common black calosoma." In the East, one is called "the fiery hunter," which is metallic green and also found in the West, and another is called "the searcher."

Our California calosoma appears to be wearing a stiff collar of the last century. Its antennae are set off to the side of the head and its heavy jaws are ever on the ready to devour cutworms and armyworms. Though they will eat all caterpillars, there is some specialization among ground beetle kinds about which caterpillars they prefer. The European ground beetle was introduced into the Eastern states specifically to control the codling moth, and it does a good job climbing up into the trees.

THE UNKNOWNS

Although there are innumerable other helpful insects, only those that can be bought or that are obvious in the garden have been mentioned. Actually, there are other parasites that you can buy—some for scale insects and others that attack fly larvae in manure piles. Most of the helpful insects are known only to the professional insect ecologist who calls them by obscure Latin names. All the ordinary gardener needs to know is that he has any number of minute friends to check his foes. He has friends, that is, if he hasn't drenched his garden with pesticides for years. In that case, he will need to restock with the well-known friends. At the same time, the transition from sprays to natural gardening will be made easier by a composting system, which will help to grow vigorous plants that can tolerate a few pests until a better balance is established. Even then some host insects will have to be tolerated to keep helpful birds and insects nearby. Not that you have to sacrifice your favorite plants for the purpose. It is possible to grow decoy plants to play this role, as we will see in a later chapter.

7. Reptiles, Frogs, and Toads

Many reptiles and amphibians are helpful to the gardener, but snakes are an exception. Snakes are not really needed in a garden—a point made in the Book of Genesis. They have their place in nature, to be sure, and a few kinds eat insects, but not the snakes found in gardens. The two you are most likely to meet when down on hands and knees are gopher and garter snakes. The latter have a potential for good, in that they eat slugs and, occasionally insects. On the other hand, they eat a great number of tree frogs and toads, as well as earthworms, and these are a gardener's delight.

Gopher snakes would be of benefit if they confined themselves to mice and gophers, but they are just as likely to climb trees in search of birds' eggs or nestlings. The younger snakes also eat the helpful lizard. The gopher snake has a habit of vibrating its tail when disturbed, so that at a quick glance, or when partly concealed by leaves, it somewhat resembles a rattler. It makes no friendly companion.

Of snakes in general, it may be said that too much of their diet consists of frogs, toads, and lizards, all of which are needed in the garden. But there is no need to grab the nearest shovel and kill the snake that happens in. You can carry it off some distance and release it, or if you don't like to do this, there is sure to be a small boy in the neighborhood who would be delighted to gather up your snake for a biology class or for a pet.

LIZARDS

Some people also have a strong aversion to lizards, though it is hard to know why. None of the standard-size lizards in this country is in the least poisonous, despite popular belief. Many are friendly little fellows, often seen sunning themselves on a tree trunk during a break in their insect-hunting. There are innumerable kinds of lizards, many species living in desert and waste places, outside the gardener's ken. Some do inhabit cultivated land where they can be of great help.

The fence lizard can be used as an example, since most gardeners will know it. Many people call this the "blue-bellied" lizard, a name that

Toads are nocturnal feeders and eat any insect that moves. We have dozens in the garden; some are pets. *Joyce R. Wilson photo* 63

describes it well. This small fellow, only two or three inches long, is a master adapter that is happy anywhere from sea level to 9,000 feet. It is often found in domestic surroundings, where garden sheds, woodpiles, stacks of lumber and the like provide good fields for his insect-hunting. The fence lizard works in the daytime and climbs trees with speed and ease. It eats grasshoppers, flies, ants, wasps, caterpillars, moths, all kinds of beetles, spiders, snails, millipedes, leafhoppers, and aphids. You could hardly improve on the list for helpfulness. "Swift," as it is sometimes called, has another trait which endears it to children. It is easily snared by a noose of thread on the end of a stick. Once caught, a few strokes on its belly relax the little lizard, and it seems to go to sleep. I'm not sure why this fascinates the young, but it starts a bond between child and reptile which may extend to the rest of nature.

There is another reptile deserving of mention. Known to most people as the horned toad, it is actually a squat lizard with decorative, harmless armor. Horned lizards are insectivorous, eating beetles, grasshoppers, and caterpillars. They occur in most states west of the Mississippi, though they prefer the drier sections.

If you live where horned lizards will thrive, it is worthwhile to add a few to the garden area. This is simply done, as they move slowly and can be picked up with ease. Keep in mind that they don't like damp situations, so put them around the margins of your garden in the waste places, and in the dry grass. There they will intercept insect foes heading your way.

FROGS

One may not care for reptiles of any kind, whether snake or lizard, but it is hard to dislike a tree frog or a cricket frog. These are the frogs that are useful in gardens. The mature frogs of these small species will feed on the ground, on a tree trunk, or even sitting lightly on a leaf. Occasionally you will see a tiny emerald gem of a tree frog in the daytime; usually, though, their presence in the garden is known by the nightly chorus.

Some frogs can live at a considerable distance from any real body of water, even though they must have at least roadside puddles in which eggs are laid and tadpoles raised in the spring. Of course, they prefer to have water nearby, and large frogs will also live in the garden if you provide a pond. In addition to providing a pool or two, you can also increase frog numbers by raising their pollywogs to maturity. If you choose a batch with legs already developed, you can turn them loose in some moist spot in the garden, where many will survive.

TOADS

The most useful member of either the amphibians or the reptiles is that ugly character the toad. Some toads hop about, but ours in the West grow so fat that they have to crawl. Toads are nocturnal feeders, night walkers. Most songbirds eat during the daylight hours, just as the fence lizard does, so we particularly need this insect-eater who works while we sleep.

Toads are especially fond of the small slugs that infest lawns and other parts of gardens where moisture lies. Of course, slugs are not insects, but they are pests, nonetheless. Toads are equally fond of cutworms, which also work at night, as you sometimes notice in the morning. Toads will eat just about any pest that moves about during the dark hours. They do eat earthworms, but that is their reward for staying around in the leaner seasons. This suggests that raising and adding additional earthworms to compost and garden is a wise move. Among other benefits, the extra supply of worms will help your toads to survive through sparse times.

There are more than a dozen kinds of toads
in this country. The common ones belong to two
species: the one in the West is called *Bufo boreas,*
and its Eastern counterpart is *Bufo terrestris.*
These toads are able to hibernate during the winter
by burrowing underground or otherwise hiding.
In the spring they come out hungry. Since they
generally live for at least four seasons, it is a good
thing to encourage them and increase their
numbers when you can.

The Western toad keeps up his work as long
as the temperature stays above 37 degrees, so it
is able to do winter clean-up on warm damp nights.
While toads are amphibians, most of their time
is spent on land. Once a year, they have to lay their
eggs in water. Any shallow water will do, including
muddy roadside pools a few inches deep.
Thousands of eggs are deposited in two strings,
after which they are left to chance. Not many
pollywogs live to shed their tail. Many birds and
animals relish them, and often the transient pools
dry up, stranding them before they are
able to breathe.

In Europe, farmers increase the toad population
in their gardens by buying mature individuals
in the market. In my experience these grown-ups
miss their old home and may depart like homing
pigeons. The best method I have found is to
collect the tadpoles when they are nearly mature,
after the legs have appeared. Here, that is likely to
be in June.

These nearly mature tadpoles are then put
in a shallow container of water. The clay dishes used
under flower pots are excellent for this
purpose. These are placed on the ground,
and in only a few days miniature toads will hop
forth. Many of them survive, for I have seen literally
hundreds of fingernail-size toads crossing the lawn
at night after such a planting. These will not
leave your garden.

8. Steps to Take Before Using Poisons

For many years it has been said insistently that one should have a "regular spray program." Garden magazines, commentators, and often garden books have been much at fault in selling this slogan to gardeners of every kind. What the slogan means is that one should spray throughout the garden in the various seasons with a whole series of poisonous sprays, whether or not anything seems to be amiss. Many gardeners follow this advice, and even more reach for a can of they-know-not-what at the first sign of any insect.

The handiness of the aerosol can has made many people forget that there are also mechanical types of insect control that work well in conjunction with the biological controls, and involve no use of poisons. Some of these methods are extremely effective, which is seldom the case with a spray. The famous pelargonium hybridizer William E. Schmidt recently told me that one can expect that only 25 to 75 percent of the surfaces to be covered will actually receive the spray or dust, even when applied by professionals in a nursery.

HANDPICKING

Handpicking certainly is primitive, but it can also be very effective, as anyone knows who keeps the caterpillars of sphinx moths off his tomato vines by this simple process. The same method can also be used when caterpillars come in great numbers rather than singly.

It is not necessary to wait until caterpillars hatch to use handpicking. If you know your plants and their pests, it is often possible to destroy the eggs. On leafy plants like chard or mustard, take a stick and run it along the garden row, exposing the undersides of the leaves. Pick off and destroy the leaves where egg clusters are found. In orchards, the eggs of the apple tree tent caterpillar are laid in a cluster that rings a branch, with several hundred eggs in each varnished ring. Since they remain there until spring, you can pick off the entire cluster as a part of pruning operations.

Some insect pests even cooperate with this method of control. The white-marked tussock moth, which is a serious pest to both shade and apple trees, almost asks you to destroy its egg clusters. The wingless female lays up to 500 eggs on the old cocoon and then covers this with a white frothy material. Since the eggs are laid in July, a gardener has until the following May to gather the clusters.

A process closely related to handpicking is

A stick run along a row of vegetables will expose the undersides of leaves.
When insect egg-clusters are found, the leaf can be picked and burned.
Joyce R. Wilson photo

Opposite
The tip of a young plum that has been cut to remove tent caterpillars. *Joyce R. Wilson photo*

to tap or shake a plant gently, or in the case of trees, to jar them with force. Certain pests of row crops defend themselves by dropping to the ground the moment they are disturbed. Among those that use this defense are diabrotica, or cucumber beetles, and various weevils.

To take advantage of this habit, all that is needed is a saucepan of water with enough soap to make a froth. With weevils you don't even need the soap, but for diabrotica the froth catches them before they can fly off (they are alert enough to change their mind even while falling). The leaves of chard, eggplant, gourds, and others are tapped while the pan is held underneath. You won't get all of them the first time, but after two or three passes, few will be left.

Both tussock moth and tent caterpillar larvae have a tendency to fall to the ground if their tree is jarred. To control them, a sticky band is placed around the lower part of the tree trunk so that the caterpillars can't crawl back into the tree. In a home garden, you can step on them to eliminate them when they are on the ground.

Another way to control tent caterpillars is to burn the nests. The inexpensive propane torch used in the home workshop is effective when only a few trees are involved.

THE VACUUM INSECT NET

Control of insect pests in this way is probably still in the future for most of us, but the results are so promising that the method should be considered. The vacuum net is the modern scientific counterpart of handpicking. Essentially it is a very powerful vacuum cleaner that sucks up insects and mites. There are wheel models that can be attached to a tractor's power takeoff for sweeping a whole field. Of more interest to a nurseryman or home gardener are some small models that were developed for taking samples to find out how many pests were present, and what helpful insects were feeding on them.

The smallest of these vacuum nets weighs only fifteen pounds and can be held in one hand. A two-cycle, one-horsepower motor creates strong suction, which draws the insects into a nylon organdy net. It is very appealing to think of going down a row of garden vegetables or along a greenhouse bench with this vacuum and simply sucking off all the pests. It wouldn't matter that the process would have to be repeated, because there would be no residue or buildup.

I have never used one of these machines, for they are still rather costly, but I did adopt the principle of the vacuum net. I have a favorite houseplant on the kitchen windowsill—an odd pelargonium that looks like a few carrots carrying umbrellas and is called "old-man-live-forever." It gets whitefly from time to time, and is so sensitive to even mild treatments that it will simply shed all its leaves.

With the vacuum net in mind, I tried our ordinary household vacuum cleaner. Holding the tube in one hand, I brushed the leaves to stir the pests into the air and proceeded to suck them up. It worked quite well except that the slender tube kept me from pulling in many whiteflies at once. My next project is a cup-shaped head about four inches in diameter.

WATER AND SOAP

One of the most effective ways of removing aphids is to wash them off with a water spray. The process is simply a matter of adjusting the nozzle to the point where it will wash the pest off. This method is most useful for houseplants, since you can take the pots out to some gravel or cement and wash off both aphids and whitefly.

69

Above
A band of Tanglefoot, or a homemade substitute, will keep caterpillars and ants from going up a trunk or limb. Below this band is santolina, an aromatic plant repugnant to insects. *Joyce R. Wilson photo*

Opposite
To remove aphids from plants, dunk them in soapy water and then rinse in a clear spray. Use only old-fashioned soap, not detergents. *Joyce R. Wilson photo*

You can set them out of the sun and repeat the process the next day before bringing them back into the house.

Water also helps to control aphids in another way. In hot weather a well-watered plant will suffer much less damage from them than one that is too dry. So in hot weather, plants that are subject to aphids should be watered generously.

A little soap added to the water usually destroys red spider and it is effective against aphids, whitefly, mealybug, and to some extent, scale insects. If you had a grandmother with a window full of houseplants, it is likely that you have watched the process. Fingers were placed over the soil to keep it from falling out, then the pot was inverted and the plant dunked in the soapy broth a few times. After that, it was rinsed clean in fresh water.

Such a shampoo does not harm even delicate plants. Keep in mind that it must be soap, not detergent. The old formula was a one-pound bar of hard laundry soap, dissolved in a little boiling water, then added to five gallons of water. While laundry soap is hard to obtain these days, there are still facial soaps that are without detergents, and it is fairly easy to make your own soap if you like trying out old ways.

Both mealybugs and scale insects can be controlled by the soapy-water process if you will do some rubbing and scraping as well. The soapy water seems to loosen their grip, so that mealybugs come off rather easily. However, for scale insects on woody plants such as camellias, I also scrape the bark lightly with a dull knife. Then, of course, the plant should be rinsed with fresh water.

STICKY BANDS AND STIFF COLLARS

Flightless insects have to crawl up onto a tree or shrub, unless they were born there, and

71

even some that were born there must travel from one part of the tree to another as a part of their life cycle. For example, codling moth caterpillars either migrate to other limbs or come down the trunk to the ground. To intercept these pests in their journeys, sticky bands attached to plant stems can be most effective. If you have washed flightless aphids from a favorite rose, a sticky band will keep them from returning to that plant. A band will also keep ants from carrying aphids into any shrub or tree that is protected by bands.

The original sticky band was made of equal parts of pine tar and molasses, and that is still an excellent formula. If you don't want to get into anything that messy, there are commercial versions, such as Tanglefoot, that can be squeezed from a tube. Various roofing tars and mastics will also work if you want to make your own barriers. The liquid roofing tars or cements—which you can buy in a small can—are best applied by dipping a small cotton clothesline rope into the tar and tying this around the tree. There is also a tape that is sticky on one side.

It helps somewhat to know what pest you are after when using sticky bands. Cankerworms will be going up the tree to lay their eggs. Rose beetles will be going up stalks, but only to feed. Other insects will be coming down. In any case, these barriers are effective and you get to see the results.

The sticky principle has a wider application than just on bands, as, for example, in flypaper. For vegetable gardens, use small sections of screen, painted with the same molasses and pine tar mix. Hang some of these, and fix others horizontally, both near the ground. The latter will pick up leafhoppers, diabrotica, and sometimes the various flea beetles. A dangling, sticky screen will collect all manner of gnats and other ephemeral creatures that drift about the garden in

swarms. With the various tangle-foot traps, there is always the worry that you may be picking up beneficial insects as well as pests. Fortunately you can check on this.

Another simple mechanical device that will prevent damage—especially by cutworms—is a collar slipped over the young plant, vine, or tree and buried a little in the soil. A milk carton cut off at each end is excellent for the purpose. Cutworms are not able to scale the waxed walls, and even rabbits are usually kept away until the plant has a good start. If you don't have enough milk cartons, ordinary roofing paper will do as well. Roll a ten-inch section into a cylinder, and put a rubber band or a string around it.

TRAPPING INSECTS WITH LIGHTS

Night-flying insects can be caught in light traps. While many that are caught are harmless to the garden, they can spoil a backyard cookout. Light traps are also helpful in a greenhouse, because you can eliminate most of the moths before they lay their eggs on the plants.

The moths of cutworms and armyworms are trapped commercially by the use of a bright light, such as a Coleman lantern or acetylene light, mounted above a large pan of waste oil. A home version is a lantern hung over a shallow pan containing water and a float of kerosene. When I collected insects as a youngster, we used an electric light bulb with a screen cone that fitted into a jar. Many nocturnal insects fell or worked their way down this funnel and were collected from the jar beneath.

Modern insect traps have made two advances: the addition of a fan, and the use of black light. A simple model with a fan is called a "Florida bug trap." It uses an ordinary hundred-watt bulb, with a small motor and fan. The electric fan draws

To protect against cutworms, a collar of ordinary tar paper is effective.
Sections of milk cartons can also be used. *Joyce R. Wilson photo*

the bugs into a removable cloth bag so that one can find out what is being caught. That is a pleasure for the children as well as instructive to the gardener.

For those who don't care about the informational aspect, there is a trap with two fine wires that are invisible when in motion. When moths flutter through these blades, they are minced and fall to the ground. For this purpose, a black light rather than an incandescent bulb is used. The "black light," which is invisible to the human eye, is an ultraviolet light particularly attractive to many night-flyers.

Many of the new traps that combine both the fan and black light principle are designed to be both compact and attractive enough to hang near a house or ornamental garden. They are rather expensive, costing about $35 to $40. The cost of a larger ultraviolet light tube is less than $2, so the handy gardener can save money by making a device of his own for parts of the garden that don't show. One standard type for orchard or field crops consists of three light tubes, with a fan above to blow the insects down a screen funnel into a five-gallon can, where they are drowned.

OTHER TRAPS

There are electric grid traps that electrocute pests as they fly between the wires. Unfortunately, they do so with a noise like a "zip," which after a while can be as annoying as the insect itself. Still, they are useful in certain situations, such as for controlling flies in dairy barns. Sometimes these electric grids are combined with light traps, but there is no real need for that.

There are simpler traps—and these the gardener will use most often. Earwigs are easily trapped in short pieces of plastic hose. These short pieces are scattered about the garden where earwig work is detected, and during the day the traps are picked up and knocked into a bucket of water. I use nothing but water, since ground beetles will also take refuge in the tubes, and I don't want to lose any of the beetles.

Some people use a hollow bamboo segment for the same purpose. An equally good, if less aesthetically pleasing, trap can be made by folding a short piece of building paper three or four times. When this is pressed flat by hand, there will be enough resilience left in the paper to form thin crevices that are irresistible to earwigs and sow bugs.

Snails are mollusks rather than insects and are, thus, more nearly related to the earthworm than the cutworm. They are, nonetheless, serious pests in the garden. Snails and small shell-less slugs can level a whole bed of zinnia seedlings in a night or two. They can also shear off every violet leaf in the spring.

Snails are attracted to moist places and any kind of shelter during the day. A few cabbage leaves scattered on moist ground in the garden will attract them. Baits containing metaldehyde are used against these pests, and these have a fair reputation if fluorides have not been added to make them more potent. Another word of caution: these baits look just like kibbled pet food and should be used with great care—some accidental deaths have been reported.

Perhaps these methods of handpicking, spraying with water, trapping, and the like seem more work than the use of poison sprays. Actually, they are not. When one strolls through a garden, he pulls a weed here and there, ties back a branch perhaps, picks off a caterpillar, or sets a trap where some damage is seen. Unlike toxic sprays, this method of control will produce no new strains of resistant superbugs, and it will deter many of the old-fashioned pests that we are used to handling.

9. The Safer Poison Sprays and Dusts

This will be a short chapter, because there aren't many poisons that can be recommended, even with qualifications. However, there may come a day when the gardener has tried all the nonpoisonous remedies and is still confronted with an insect problem.

This can happen when some new pest arrives in the garden, and no natural enemies have appeared yet to combat it. Pests migrate, like other creatures, and it is a rule of biology that newly arrived species are initially very successful. We know the story of such imported pests as the codling moth, San Jose scale, boll weevil, and the Mediterranean fruit fly. There are local migrations, as well—the spread of Colorado potato beetle being an example. Once this pest lived on a Western native plant called buffalo bur; at about the time of the Civil War, it crossed the Mississippi and traveled to the East and South.

The home gardener will seldom face such wholesale invasions, but from time to time new pests may arrive, or an old enemy may have an especially good year. Instead of normal numbers that are kept in bounds by normal controls, there may be myriads of pests. Such cycles are normal in all forms of animal life.

If the time comes when some part of your garden needs emergency measures, there are a few relatively safe kinds of spray ingredients to look for. The safer sprays fall into two groups, the

Pyrethrum, the daisy-like flower which when dried and powdered is a powerful insect killer. *USDA photo*

botanicals and the organic phosphates.
I use the comparative form "safer" because some of them are not safe at all, and others are only safe in the sense that they do not persist as long as the more dangerous poisons discussed in Chapter I. Any spray, to be effective, has to be toxic to something, so we must use them with caution.

THE BOTANICALS

Botanicals are derived from substances in plants. In a sense, they are thus natural, and some people take this to mean they are intrinsically safe. That is not the case at all. A number of plants— datura, henbane, belladonna, and others— contain alkaloids that are very deadly poisons, especially if concentrated. Some of these also have uses in medicine, but that is beyond our discussion.

Nicotine, which is extracted from tobacco plants, is one of these alkaloids. A spray made of nicotine sulfate is often recommended as a substitute for the chlorinated hydrocarbons. It is effective against aphids, thrips, and leafhoppers. It comes in the form of a concentrate to be diluted, or as a powder to be burned for fumigating greenhouses. In the hands of experts, it may be useful for the latter purpose, but I can see no reason why a home gardener should keep such dangerous stuff around the house. Besides, there are many other ways to control this particular group of insects.

I have found one use for ordinary, unconcentrated nicotine that I think is safe, and certainly is preferable to the standard alternative. The soil mealybug can be a difficult pest to remove from the garden. It looks like a sprinkling of moldy white powder at the roots of a plant. The prescribed remedy for soil mealybug is aldrin, but that is one of the most persistent of the chlorinated hydrocarbons. A good substitute is old tobacco buried in the soil above the spot of infestation. When this is watered in, enough of the nicotine leaches out to destroy the colony. (We also use other natural methods to control soil mealybugs. In our area, wild dock seems to be the host plant. Dock is an acid-lover with a long, fleshy rootstalk, so we lime the soil to keep the dock out.)

For house plants subject to mealybugs, African violets being particularly susceptible, an infusion of tobacco can be made by soaking some cheap tobacco in water—at the rate of one pound to four gallons of water. Any chewing or pipe tobacco will do for the purpose, and it is much cheaper than aldrin.

Pyrethrin and Rotenone. These two plant-derived substances are the most useful of all the safer sprays. One or the other, or a combination of both, should be thought of first when you are in need of a spray. Remember to read the label, if you are buying the spray. The manufacturer is all too likely to have added a "kicker" to this combination to give more lasting effects. Methoxychlor seems to be the present favorite, and, while it is not the worst possible additive, it takes away all the advantages of the safer twins.

Both pyrethrin and rotenone are toxic to certain insects but are harmless to warm-blooded animals—which means that they won't harm people, pets, or birds. The Master Nurserymen's Association long ago recognized this safety factor and put out a product for nursery use called "Bonanza." The nurseryman, unlike most food producers, must meet his customers face-to-face.

Pyrethrin occurs in the flowers, and especially in the developing seeds, of a plant called pyrethrum, which resembles the painted daisy. Since pyrethrin is effective against flies, it makes a good livestock spray. In the house it is also effective against roaches and bedbugs.

For those who would like to grow their own insecticide, the "insect powder plant" is *Chrysanthemum cinerariaefolium.* Few seedsmen in this country carry the seeds, but you can get them from Thompson & Morgan in England, and, probably, also from specialists here. The plant requires a warm location and good drainage—a south slope with gravelly soil is ideal for this hardy perennial. Commercially, the plants are grown in Kenya, Tanzania, and Ecuador, where they are set a foot apart in rows spaced at 3-foot intervals, but a gardener can find a more attractive arrangement than that.

Inside the house, pyrethrin can be recommended with no qualifications. In the garden it has one limitation: it is just as effective on ladybugs as on diabrotica or aphids, so the gardener should take care. On ornamental plants and shrubs, it is usually possible to examine the field closely before spraying. If aphids are the problem and ladybugs are feeding on them, wait. If you see no ladybugs, go ahead and spray.

As mentioned before, rotenone is another botanical that is often combined with pyrethrin. They make an excellent pair, since the latter is more effective against caterpillars and has a repelling quality that lasts for three days. While this doesn't kill the insects, it keeps them off the plant. Again, if you are buying sprays, it will be necessary to read the fine print to make sure the manufacturer hasn't added some other ingredients.

The substance rotenone is contained in the roots of a number of tropical trees and climbing plants, doubtless for their own protection against insects. Derris powder, which comes from a root in the East Indies, contains this substance. It is effective against true bugs.

In the United States, the weed called "devil's shoestring" contains rotenone. Where these grow locally, it might be worthwhile to dry and pulverize a few of the weeds to test the powder for effectiveness.

Other Botanicals. A powder made from hellebore is an old and tried weapon against the larvae of various sawflies, such as the rose slug. The powder can be mixed with ordinary limestone and used as a dust for these maggots, or for the root maggots of cabbage and cauliflower, or one ounce can be dissolved in a quart of boiling water, then another quart of water added before applying it to the soil.

Quassia is another old remedy, particularly for aphids. It is an alkaloid of great bitterness. Derived from a Jamaican tree, it is available in the form of wood chips or shavings. Soak 1¾ pounds of the chips in 12 gallons of water for 24 hours. Formerly, soap, which in itself is a very good and safe insecticide, was often added. (But by no means use detergent, as that is something else altogether, as explained in the previous chapter. Use old-fashioned laundry soap, or fish-oil soap if you can find it.)

It is somewhat out of context to be speaking of soap under the heading of botanicals, but soaps were often used and proved effective even by themselves. The rate was one pound of laundry soap to five gallons of water. This formula is still one of the best for houseplants and for certain of the aphid attacks outside, as well as for various sawfly maggots.

One new botanical that is getting attention is ryania, which is made from a shrub of the same name that grows in Trinidad. The mild alkaloid it contains doesn't kill insects, it incapacitates them. A bug that is feeling ill is obviously a better bug from the gardener's point of view, and in the strictly competitive bug world, the sickly one won't last.

ORGANIC PHOSPHATES

There is a small group of synthetic chemicals that still has a good reputation for garden and household use. These are the organic phosphates. Organic in this usage is a chemical term; it has nothing to do with "organic" in the sense of a philosophy of gardening or farming. There are three members of the group that the gardener is likely to hear about: Malathion, Dibrom, and Diazinon.

Malathion is the least toxic to humans, but its range of effectiveness is mainly against aphids, leafhoppers, and thrips. While it is always recommended as the safest for vegetable crops, there is a drawback to be kept in mind. According to the USDA Farmers' Bulletin #2148, Malathion "will intensify smog damage to table beets, spinach and certain types of leaf lettuce." What we have run into here is "synergistic" effect: the picture is altered when one more factor is added. The chemical formula of spray plus smog is not so simple as that of the spray alone.

Dibrom is morbid spelled backwards. It is effective against lawn moths, cutworms, and other caterpillars, earwigs, scale, mealybugs, and mites. It is only moderately toxic to humans, so it might be called upon for use in the flower garden when special problems arise.

Diazinon, the third organic phosphate, is difficult to evaluate. It is highly toxic, but it is also effective against a wide range of insects. When we name it among the "safer" sprays, we definitely have to qualify that. In January of 1970, a farm worker in Delano, California, won a judgment on the basis of the organic phosphate poisoning that the field workers are consistently exposed to. The effect of the poison was to reduce the victim's blood enzyme (cholinesterase) level to a dangerously low point. The doctor told this victim that he couldn't work again for five months.

Diazinon breaks down in from ten to twelve days, depending upon the crop to which it is applied. During that time, it is dangerous to humans. Hence, it could scarcely be recommended for the home vegetable garden where it is likely to drift to other rows of vegetables. It might find a place on fruit early in the season, or on ornamentals. But one should remember that Diazinon can be absorbed directly through the skin in harmful quantities.

DORMANT OIL SPRAY

Miscible oils, such as Volck, are often recommended by organic gardeners. They are definitely nonpoisonous. When applied to fruit trees during the leafless period, the light oil and water mix kills insect eggs that are overwintering on the bark. General and widespread use, as with fogging machines, is open to the same objections that I have made to such use of the other sprays: it will kill some of your insect friends as well.

The best way to use oil sprays is in specific cases. Oil will take care of scale and mites on particular shrubs and, if used carefully, will not damage leaves. Spray should be confined to the limbs where the scale is. If you spray leaves of ornamentals for mites, a very dilute oil must be used, and only on the underside of leaves, and out of the sun. Otherwise, the leaves will burn, which is no better than the effect of red spider.

LIME AND SULFUR

My views on this pair seems to be heretical, since most books on organic gardening claim that the combination is an obnoxious poison not to be used. Probably the idea began in the old days when lime sulfur was used as a base for Paris green and lead arsenate sprays. By themselves, both lime and sulfur are natural chemicals that have value in soil fertility.

Sulfur is an excellent fungicide that is used to control mildew. It will also deter mites, aphids, and cutworms. Sulfur is a little tricky to use, as the finer forms will burn plants if applied in too much quantity, or when the temperature is too high. To be safe, use only the simplest sulfur, and avoid forms like "special electric" which are very volatile. My neighbors use a little lime and sulfur to dust young cabbages and broccoli. A mild mix discourages aphids and worms and allows the young plants to get ahead of the pests. In the happy times before DDT, the same mix was used on grapevine buds to very good effect, and vines are still sulfured for mildew.

Lime is the only ingredient in old-fashioned whitewash. Its insect-repelling quality and its value for killing eggs on fruit trees is about equal to that of dormant oil spray. On young trees, whitewash has the additional advantage of protecting against sunburn.

AVOIDING POISONS

Remember that the aim is a poison-free garden using natural controls as a check. None of the poisons listed here should be used if you can avoid using them. Try to think of other measures first; it is surprising how seldom you will need the poisons. When trouble does arise, use the nonpoisonous materials first, next the safer botanicals, selected for a particular target pest, and only lastly the safer synthetics. These will affect natural controls, so instead of using them it is a good idea to give some thought to long-range changes in garden practice. Some of these changes might tip the balance in the gardener's favor.

Some safe insect killers and retardants. *Joyce R. Wilson photo*

10. Companion Plantings and Trap Plants

It makes a great difference where a plant is grown in a garden: some plants like to be next to each other, while others are offended by certain company. Some plants are more attractive to insects. It is possible to take advantage of these facts to protect more delicate or more valuable kinds.

The idea that plants respond to the company they keep is very old and sounds like folklore, but not all information on this subject comes from the old herbals. There is a current research grant to finance scientific study to find out more about why certain plants like to grow together.

Dr. F. W. Went, head of the Laboratory of Desert Biology of the University of Nevada, discovered that many annual wild flowers, among them desert chicory and fiddle-neck, grew much more lushly near shrubs. The increased growth—which was from two to ten times as great— had nothing to do with shade, since Dr. Went found that even dead shrubs had the same stimulating effect. He surmised that the extra growth was the result of organic matter captured by the shrub and held in the thin skin of the desert soil. Detritus blown by desert winds is caught by shrubs, whether living or not, and returned to the soil near the shrub by the activity of fungus. No organic gardener would object to this explanation, since it confirms the fact that organic matter returned to the soil is transformed by the action of fungi and bacteria into readily available plant food—hence, the lush wild flowers, even on desert sand. Generally, however, it is a different kind of mutual relationship that the organic gardener has in mind when he speaks of companion plantings. He is thinking of the principle of intermixing plants as protection from insects.

Opposite
Companion planting and trap plants are used extensively here; healthy growth and colorful flowers are plentiful.
Richard F. Conrat photo

82

84

COMPANION PLANTINGS

Some plants repel insects and other pests.
Probably the best-known example is the nasturtium.
It has been claimed for many years that if you
plant nasturtiums, aphids will be no problem. Dr.
Kring of the Connecticut Agricultural Experiment
Station ran a series of tests by interplanting
cabbages and nasturtiums. There was a repelling
factor, and he concluded that it was the orange
color of the blossoms.

Insects can be affected by colors, sounds, and
smells. The same scientists found that the color
yellow, curiously enough, attracts aphids, so he
devised a trap that was colored yellow and coated
with a sticky substance.

It is always interesting to try out garden theories,
no matter how unusual they sound, and for years
I have grown masses of nasturtiums among the
vegetables. Nothing looks better than their fiery
blooms peeking around from behind the dark-green
leaves of zucchini squashes. I also have the climbing
nasturtium *Tropaeolum lobbianum* growing on the
sides of the garden shed. These climbers make
their way inside the shed through cracks and, as
they are perennials though seldom grown as such,
they bloom inside, brightening many a dark winter
day. There are few aphids among the vegetables
and perhaps nasturtiums are the reason, though
it should be added that there are also ladybugs
and lacewings working on the problem.

Companion plantings work on the principle of
intermixing plants certain pests don't like, along
with those that they like all too well. It is obviously
good garden practice to mix up plantings. Spreading
herbs among the vegetables, or garlic among flower
beds, will, at the very least, break up the appeal
to pests. A garden set all to one kind of plant is a
sure target for its particular pests. In mixed plantings,
the pests are less likely to build into epidemic
proportions.

Euphorbia has a splendid reputation among many
of my friends and neighbors as a repellent for both
insects and gophers. A variegated leaf variety of
euphorbia that is often called "gopher plant"
contains a milky juice which is poisonous and is
particularly effective on mucous membranes.
Certainly no gopher would eat the plant and poison
himself, and many euphorbias scattered through the
garden may discourage the pest. In any case,
the variegated forms are attractive visually and
can be tucked here and there with benefit.

Herbs. Some herbs are effective in fending off
insect attacks. Many of them are immune to attack
themselves, and a few will discourage insects over
a wider area if interplanted.

The one with the best reputation in this respect
is tansy. Common tansy is a coarse wildling that
grows too tall to be attractive in most parts of the
garden, but it can be fitted into perennial borders
and backgrounds. Fern-leaf tansy is altogether
good with its dark-green divided leaves and bright
buttons. There is no doubt that both forms of
tansy are strong insect repellents.

Tansy was used as a "strewing herb" in medieval
times, when floors of both cottages and castles
were covered with straw. Insects and other
arthropods, such as mites, were at least as
abundant as today, and repellents were scattered
in with the straw. Tansy was one of the herbs
most used. For anyone who wants to experiment
with homemade insecticides, by using juices or
powders concocted from herbs, tansy is the plant
to begin with.

My own favorite for companion plantings is
rue. No insect will have anything to do with this
bitter plant. In former times clusters of rue were
hung in the house to repel flies. Today I plant it
at my greenhouse door in hopes that it will flag
down some unwanted pest, and here and there in

the garden where the much-divided blue foliage is an excellent foil for any color of bloom.

There are other medicinal herbs that are worth trying for companion plantings, as they have vermifuge value and are also a delight to brush against when working in the garden. The most promising are:

feverfew
southernwood and other artemsias
lavender
pyrethrum daisy
chamomile
pennyroyal and other mints (kept in control)

Even the culinary herbs are for the most part free from insect attacks, so I plant rows of summer savory and clumps of marjoram and thyme in between and among the rows of vegetables, as well as here and there throughout the flower garden. At the very least, the aromatic scents make work on a warm day a matter of pleasure, and perhaps they also provide a canopy of protection to the plants around them.

Onions and Garlic. Onions have many attackers, including thrips and more than one kind of maggot. When they are planted in long graveyard-like rows, the pests can simply travel from one onion plant to the next. To prevent these pests from proceeding straight up the rows, like mourners on Memorial Day, a mixed planting is advisable. It will also prevent the building up of some kinds of harmful fungi that affect onions.

I have never found pests on garlic, even though I have on occasion planted extensive plots. It is said that planting a ring of garlic around fruit trees will save them from borers. That may be true, and it is certain that gophers and soil insects do not attack garlic. So it may provide a protective screen about other plants and will certainly provide a family supply of the bulbs.

TRAP PLANTS

Probably the name "decoy plants" would better describe what is involved in this type of insect control, but the professionals have always spoken of "trap plants." The concept is nearly the opposite of that just discussed, and there is a good deal more scientific information available on the effectiveness of the method. The basic aim here is to attract insects rather than to repel them, and for that purpose a crop of less value to the gardener is used to lure pests away from the major planting.

An example would be in the control of the squash-vine borer, which does most of its damage against winter squash and pumpkins. The rows may be interplanted with summer squash; then, when the borers have made their way into these vines, the summer squash is dug up and burned. The advantage of trap plants over those that repel is that they work over a large area, whereas the repelling factors of aromatic oil or color do not work far from the plants to be protected. Trap plants acting as hosts to pests will draw them from the whole area.

Ways of adapting trap planting to the vegetable garden are not difficult to devise. One commercial practice that can be borrowed is the use of corn plantings to protect tomatoes and cotton. It happens that the tomato fruitworm, the bollworm, and the corn earworm are all the same insect, *Heliothis*. It prefers to eat the silk of the corn and will seek it out in preference to the tomato fruit. In large plantings, a row of corn is set around the tomato field, but in the home garden a few hills can be planted in succession near the plot to be protected. It is much easier to detect and destroy the worms on the corn silk than to find them underneath your ripening tomatoes.

Clover and alfalfa are also attractive to bollworms —and to aphids. A patch of either of these legumes planted nearby will lure pests from the main garden.

Clover and alfalfa have the additional advantages of adding nitrogen to the soil and of being perfect for composting at the end of the season.

Cabbage and other cold crops are attacked by aphids, and a cabbage head affords them good protection. But there are parasites that feed on these aphids, and one can combine protection for the parasite with a trap crop by planting Texas leaf mustard near the cabbage plants. The mustard carries the parasite through the season; and on its loose leaves the aphid is much easier to control, either with a safe spray or dust, or simply by composting the infested plants.

For fruit trees and small orchards, a cover crop acts as a decoy by supplying an alternate host for many insects. It also provides extra food for beneficial insects. While the lacewing is insectivorous, it can also live on certain high-protein foods, such as pollen and nectar. Any cover crop that supplies these will encourage lacewings. In California vineyards and orchards, the mustard is in full bloom by February to provide pollen and to act as a trap crop.

Not enough research has been done to make possible a listing of many specific trap plants, but an alert gardener interested in natural controls can experiment on the basis of the principle involved. Remember that for biological control it is necessary to tolerate a few pests as food for the predators. Far better that these should be on trap plants than on your flowers and vegetables.

INSECTIVOROUS PLANTS

Insect-eating plants are curious examples of the wonders of plant adaptation. They are fascinating and instructive, but are of little practical help to the gardener. Several carnivorous plants are native to the United States. For the most part, they are bog plants that require a high moisture content in the air around them, which reduces their value in other settings.

The Venus's-flytrap, which comes from the southern United States, has extraordinary jaws that snap shut when an insect crawls over them. Inside, digestive juices are released and the insect is consumed. That sounds like a good thing for ridding the house of flies. Unfortunately, however, the air in our house is kept dry—too dry for the plant—so we have to put a glass cloche or plastic bag over the flytrap. Then it loses its value as a trap and must be fed bits of meat. Outside in its habitat, this plant has a place of value, and inside it will amuse and instruct the young.

The sundew is another science-fiction plant that succeeds very well in the real world, and it is probably more useful than the flytrap. A half-dozen sundews belonging to the genus *Drosera* are grown in gardens and greenhouses here in California. They can be raised easily from seed and thrive if kept well watered. The leaves of sundews are bordered with hair-like filaments that exude a sticky glue. When an insect is entangled in this, the hairs turn inward to the center of the leaf. The liquid then becomes an acid which digests the victim. Its food value is absorbed through the leaf.

There are less complex carnivorous plants, such as the butterwort, which simply rolls up its leaves to catch an insect. Pitcher plants have a honeyed bait, and juices within its hollow leaves digest insects that fall into the pitcher. Cobra lilies have hollow bulbous traps at the tips of their leaves and insects that make their way inside are slowly transformed by decay into plant food.

Other devices are used. One of these plants uses a particularly fetid odor as bait for insects. When I raised this plant in the house, my wife remarked pointedly that the flowers were not bothered by flies. So we composted that experiment.

This carnivorous plant is the Venus's-flytrap. *Joyce R. Wilson photo*

PROPER MIXING AND PLANT ROTATION

We have seen that some plants like each other's company. Some have equally strong aversions to each other; usually this is due to competition for root-space. If you set out a number of plants with shallow, spreading roots, all will compete for the same food and moisture, leaving them weak and more subject to insect attack than plants that are growing vigorously. For this reason, a gardener should give thought to root depth and style. While this requires long-range planning, it does have an effect on insect and disease control.

Another thing to keep in mind is that rotation of plants will also retard pests and diseases. In addition, it helps soil fertility, particularly among the trace elements. Different plants require varying quantities of nutrients. Those that can send their roots down deep will bring up minerals unavailable to shallow-rooted kinds. Squashes require a great deal of nitrogen, while peas manufacture most of their own. These considerations make it wise to move plants to new settings each year.

Fruit trees and shrubs can seldom, if ever, be moved, but they can be mixed when first set out. Though there is some formal appeal in planting all apples or all pears together, this should not be done. Monoculture is an open invitation to insect pests, to virus diseases, and to fungus of a pernicious sort. When you mix plantings, you are enlisting an important natural ally in the continuing fight against your garden's enemies.

In short, keep the same kinds of plants apart whenever possible, keep similar root structures away from each other; and move annual plantings from place to place. These simple rules will not prevent pests, but they are more examples of the preventive medicine we have been describing that will make it easier to keep pests in control without the use of unacceptable poisons.

11. Plant Diseases

The home gardener who grows a variety of plants, trees, and shrubs will generally have less trouble with plant diseases than he does with insect pests. Diseases occur less frequently, and they are fairly predictable in behavior. They are likely to concentrate in certain years, in particular areas, on some kinds of soils, or on certain plants. Most diseases have a limited number of host plants—for instance, those that attack glads are not apt to attack geraniums—and they can often be controlled by proper gardening procedures or by selecting disease-resistant varieties.

There are plant societies devoted to individual plants, such as roses. You may wish to join the societies that concern themselves with those plants that you like best. They will keep you informed of what to expect and advise you of events such as the appearance of a new rust in Australia or Europe. Being forewarned, you may prevent the spread of a new disease by burning the first few leaves on which it appears.

Plant diseases are classified in three groups, according to whether they are cause by viruses, fungi, or bacteria.

VIRUSES

The virus exists somewhere between the world of life and the world of inert matter. It is composed of two nonliving substances—a protein and an acid—yet when these are combined and in contact with living cells, the virus will multiply.

Since there is no spray for combatting viruses, the gardener is forced to use other methods, such as destroying infected plants or shifting the planting to other kinds. If you suspect a virus to be at work, your local agricultural advisors and university experiment stations can help you by identifying the virus, and suggesting what plants are immune to the type of strain at hand. Many kinds of plants will not be bothered by the disease at all.

Probably the commonest virus diseases are those that resemble tobacco mosaic. The leaves develop yellow blotchiness or yellow veining. (Some of the viruses that cause net-veining seem to be perfectly harmless to the plant, and the results may even be ornamental.)

Another condition to watch for is the crisping and curling of leaves. Aphids can have a similar effect, but you will soon learn to distinguish the difference. Still another result of virus attack is spotted wilt. Though there are also a number of other reasons for a sudden wilt, this is a possible cause, and a serious one.

Isolation. Viruses can be spread by insects, or by water splashing from one plant to another. Tobacco mosaic, which affects plants other than tobacco, is said to be spread through tobacco smoke. Human hands will also spread viruses, as will cutting tools.

A virus disease is seldom, if ever, inherited through a seed generation. So whenever it is possible, grow a plant from seed rather than from cuttings. Usually we can't follow this good advice, however: a wild seedling fruit tree is of no use—we want a particular clone, and that has to be grown from a cutting.

We can only take precautions that are known to be helpful. For instance, it has been found that ordinary household bleach (sodium hypochloride) effectively sterilizes a cutting knife against the spread of citrus virus. Use a pint and a half of bleach (Clorox, Purex, etc.) to make one gallon when water is added.

Naturally, infected cuttings are kept apart, suspects destroyed, and finally a virus-free propagating stock established. The home gardener should follow this method of isolation for any plants that are mobile. More often than not, chlorotic symptoms—yellowing or blanching—will appear in pot plants rather than established perennials. It often takes as much as a year for virus symptoms to show up on new plants, so if you have a specialty, watch your new purchases carefully.

Most of the time and most happily, the symptoms will not be a virus disease at all. Food deficiency can cause very similar effects. It is now popular to grow and ship plants in "artificial soil"—usually a mixture of perlite, vermiculite, sand, and peat moss, with a dash of fertilizers added. Since the medium is very porous, these chemicals leach out of the pot or tub after the first few waterings. The starved plant will then develop yellow blotches on its leaves which look much like a virus attack. It is a good idea to isolate the plant, since it is new and may be bringing in trouble, but at the same time give it a light feeding of bone, fish, and cottonseed meal. If the plant freshens up again, the problem was not a virus.

There is a counterpart to this trouble that is caused by *too much* chemical fertilizer. This is a condition that resembles curly top—the edges of leaves are crisped and curled, and often there are brown and dry spots within the leaf. When a gardener is called for consultation, he always asks first if the plant has been fertilized recently. When the answer is yes, he then wants to know the formula. Most often it turns out to be a few shovelfuls of 20-30-20, or some similar terror. The only remedy then is to flood the plant with water in the hope of leaching away some of these chemicals.

Heat. Some viruses can be destroyed by means of heat, even a low heat if it is continuous. Rose plants placed in a room heated to 100 degrees for at least three weeks will be cured of rose virus. The virus-free plants can then be watched and selected for propagating stock. Other kinds of viruses are killed at a temperature of 160 degrees.

This fact suggests that a well-run compost pile might destroy viruses as plant material is heated in it in the process of decay. Many composters assume that they get protection from this process and throw suspect material in with the rest. My own view is that the kinds and strains of viruses are too little known to take that chance. You don't really need every last scrap of available material to make a compost heap; it is better to discard doubtful plants.

91

FUNGI

Fungi are tiny plants that lack chlorophyll. In the soil, many kinds of fungi are indispensable in transforming organic matter into plant food. Other kinds are necessary in making such things as bread, wine, cheese, and soy sauce. Unfortunately, there are also fungi that cause rust, black spot, and certain wilts. Most fungi are visible when they begin to form colonies, as with rust. Other kinds are not seen, and only their damage is visible.

There are any number of chemical fungicides on the market—in fact, the government has an entire volume devoted to their names and suggested uses. Some of these are effective, but they are not selective. That means that if much of the fungicide gets into the soil, it will destroy the beneficial fungi as well. So, if you feel that you must spray your roses for black spot and rust, put a plastic sheet on the ground underneath.

Alternative measures are once again the path to look for. It has been known for more than a hundred years that certain strains within the same kind of plant are more resistant to disease than others. For example, the red onion was immune to a blight that often became a serious disease among yellow onions. Scientists reasoned that if they could isolate the resistant gene from the red onion and introduce it into the yellow strain, the latter would be resistant, too.

This kind of work has been perfected for most of the basic food crops. No farmer today would plant any variety of wheat that was not rust resistant. Another fungus, verticillium, caused a wilt in tomatoes in some areas. This could be disastrous, as it might defoliate an entire patch. Today the gardener has only to make sure that the tomato seed he buys has been bred as a wilt-resistant strain.

Not all fungus problems have been solved in this way, however, so a gardener must use procedures. Any fungus multiplies by sending out thousands of tiny spores that float through the air. If you touch a leaf infected with gray mold, you will see a visible cloud of spores drift away, while rusts appear to cling more tightly to the leaf. In either case, it is important to arrest the disease early by picking off the leaves or buds on which the fungus appears.

Spores will lie dormant for long periods, so it is a good idea to remove fallen leaves and litter from the ground if there is trouble with rusts or molds. For mulching, you can use straw or sawdust, which will be free of the disease. When there is trouble for more than one season, the fungus has probably built up in the soil.

Shifting plants to kinds less susceptible is good practice. It requires some knowledge, since the same disease may be destructive to carnations, pansies, petunias, asters, roses, and camellias. Herbs are a good choice: many of them seem to be nearly immune to the common fungus diseases.

Damping Off and Stem Rot in Cuttings. "Damping off" is a fungus disease of seedlings. The first two leaves appear, and perhaps the first real leaves as well, then the plants rot off at the soil level. In my experience, this seldom happens except when the seedlings are growing in flats—usually out of their normal season, and inside, where the atmosphere is close. Seedlings growing in the open ground have the benefit of air circulation and sunlight, which are enemies of fungal growth. So if seedlings are placed where there is a bit of sun and air, for part of the day at least, there will be less trouble from this problem.

A sterile medium for seeds is sometimes called for if they are being grown inside and in difficult conditions. One famous seed company suggests straight peat moss as a medium.

This should be well tamped down, and the seeds covered with sterile sand. Peat moss is highly acid, which some seeds don't like, and it is also somewhat spongy. Another medium, the John Innes seedling mix—which consists of two parts fibrous loam, one part peat, and one part sand— is nearly perfect, except that it is not sterile because of the loam content. If the flats are well-placed, there will be little trouble, but if you want to take every precaution, the loam mix can be sterilized by placing it in the kitchen oven at a temperature of 180 degrees for two hours.

Cuttings may be attacked by rots due to either fungi or bacteria. A medium of sterilized sand and vermiculite prevents most of the trouble. Remember that river sand is anything but sterile. If you are adding peat moss to this mix, it should be from an ancient bed. There is a new variety produced in California which is not really peat but only partly decayed sedge. It is great for the garden, as it has a full complement of working soil organisms, but don't set cuttings in it if you want a sterile medium.

Mildew. In its first stages, downy mildew works on the surface of some plants and their fruits. Then, if unchecked, it may get into the plant cells and show itself as purple blotches along the stems. Damp weather favors this as well as other fungus diseases.

On some plants, the attack is so inevitable that one should go to work before there are any signs. In a damp year, grapevines are subject to mildew in stems, leaves, and within the clusters of grapes.

An early dusting of sulfur before mildew gets under way is a preventive. We have already warned that sulfur will burn foliage, or fail to act at all, depending upon its fineness and temperature. When too much sulfur falls into the soil, it will build up an acid condition, so it is always wise to follow with an application of lime on the soil to counteract possible overacidity.

Chemical Fungicides. There are special situations which may warrant the use of more complex fungicides—such as when a nurseryman ships a plant in what must be a nearly airless carton. Naturally the buyer doesn't want to receive a moldy batch of leaves and stems. There may also be a place for some fungicides on the cutting bench. I tried one for a while but then discovered that it had to be diluted about ten to one to prevent damage to cell tissues.

In the end, taking some precautions seems the best method of control. Space the cuttings a little farther apart, and see that the air circulation is good. This seems to work about as well and has the advantage of avoiding those unpleasant words on the label— DON'T BREATHE or WEAR CLEAN PROTECTIVE CLOTHING AND BATHE AFTER EACH EXPOSURE. The only reason to have a garden is for pleasure, and KEEP OUT OF THE REACH OF CHILDREN on a label diminishes my pleasure.

BACTERIA

Bacteria are tiny animals rather than plants. Among humans, they cause more diseases than fungi do, but on garden plants I think the opposite is true. The effects of bacteria are often the same as fungus diseases. Black rot of cabbages and similar plants are caused by a bacteria rather than a fungus. One happy difference is that bacteria are likely to die out of a given soil if it is left idle for a year or two, while fungi may stay for a long time.

Since bacteria are short-term residents, crop rotation is always the first step to take. The next is to maintain a high organic content

in the soil. Living soils contain myriads of
microscopic creatures that keep bacterial damage
to a minimum—if this were not so, our planet
would probably be as bare as the moon. One
group of these antibiotic organisms, called
actinomycetes, has endless value. A recent report
on these antibiotics requires 954 pages
simply to list their names and the diseases each
is effective against.

A great many bacterial diseases were in former
times transmitted through seeds. Today, you
almost certainly will not get infected seeds through
any standard supply.

CULTURE INDEXING

Protective organisms keep the soil creatures
in balance so that none can dominate
for long. But sometimes we need more specific
protection from bacterial and other plant diseases.
Culture indexing is an elaborate way of
selecting healthy plants and growing from these.

To make the selection, a thin slice of tissue
is taken from a number of plants and put
in a medium favorable to disease growth. Some of
the plants will show no sign of disease, and
these are then reselected by further testing. The
healthy plants are then put in a "mother
block" which is covered with cheesecloth so that
disease-bearing insects can't reach them.

For the nurseryman, these elaborate steps are
worthwhile, even though costly. For the home
gardener, the situation is somewhat different. Even
the healthiest of roses developed by these
measures will still have to encounter the
uncultured ruffians already in the garden. So once
again we fall back on the "divide and conquer"
technique. A block of roses has a traditional appeal
—to diseases and insects as well as to people.
If you will interplant roses with marigolds,
nasturtiums, geraniums, and other flowers with fewer
troubles, the display will go much better.

12. Some Specific Problems

We have talked about many ways to have a beautiful garden without using insecticides and sprays. A good soil, composts and mulching, and keeping birds and beneficial insects on the site are all part of the careful gardener's program.

Here are some problems and how to solve them, on plants such as fruit trees, ornamentals, and vegetables.

FRUIT TREES

Codling moth, tent caterpillars, railroad worms, and other caterpillars. Make three releases of trichogramma wasps—one during the budding period, one during the bloom, and one during petal drop. This can be done for as little as $15 an acre and will give nearly complete control of caterpillars without killing beneficial insects or harming birds.

Removing egg clusters: The eggs of some moths are laid as a complete band around small limbs. These can be removed as part of pruning. Others lay clusters of eggs on trunks and larger limbs. These can be scraped off and you will have 100-200 fewer moths with each cluster destroyed.

When faced with a tree full of caterpillars: Some, like the tussock moth, can be jarred from the tree by shaking it. Destroy caterpillars on the ground and place sticky bands around the trunk so none can crawl back into the tree. Tent caterpillars won't jar loose. Usually they begin at the tips of limbs; these can be pruned off. Sometimes burning the tent with a small propane torch is feasible. Use an old paint bucket filled with kerosene or waste oil and scrape caterpillars into it.

Prevention of moth build-up: Use black-light traps to catch the mature moths before they

lay eggs. (Check contents of the traps so you will know which moth to look out for next year. The major pests are not hard to identify.)
Birds that feed extensively on caterpillars: Woodpeckers; bluebirds; orioles; wrens, robins; grosbeaks; some jays and magpies; mockingbird; catbird; hermit thrush; some sparrows and juncos; titmice and chickadees.
Insects that eat caterpillars: Mature mantises eat any insect they find, including caterpillars. Several kinds of ground beetles climb trees in search of caterpillars—"the fiery hunter" (*Calosoma calidum*), "the searcher" (*Calosoma scrutator*). These natives climb trees for caterpillars. One European species has been introduced to combat the gypsy moth—*Calosoma sycophanta.* If these are seen at work (which will be at night) avoid using sticky bands since they can't fly but have to climb the tree.

The Trichogramma parasitizes moth eggs.

Control of aphids and scale insects

Ladybugs. There are several useful species— black-spotted red ladybug (*Hippodamia convergens*) and an unspotted red (*Hippodamia c. ambigua*). One gallon of these beetles contains 74,000 hungry helpers and costs about $7. One quart will do for home orchard and garden. They should be released in six or seven batches, not all at once. They need some cover until the trees are well leafed-out. Keep a cover crop in the orchard; that will keep the ladybugs at home. Don't cultivate the orchard too early.
Lacewings (Chrysopa carnea). These are equally effective against aphids and scale. They are more difficult to raise so the cost is a little higher to begin with, but if you don't spray, they multiply. Insectary-raised eggs cost $1 per hundred.
Small birds that thrive on aphids and scale. Among these are: warblers; titmice; wrens; flycatchers; gnatcatchers.

Argentine ants carry aphids into trees where they protect them in order to get the honeydew extracted by aphids, scale, and whitefly. They may carry whole colonies of black cherry aphids into the trees. Sticky bands will prevent them from climbing into trees. Bone meal is effective against their nests in the ground.

Control of mites. These are minute non-insect pests that suck the sap. "Red spider" is one variety. An invisible parasite keeps them under control when the trees are not sprayed with poisons that kill the parasite. Mites thrive when the undersides of leaves are covered with dust. Avoid dust in orchards and spray the undersides of leaves with plain water in gardens. For orchards, a novel remedy is a mixture of wheat flour (20 pounds to 100 gallons of water plus a half-gallon of buttermilk). This glues the mites to a leaf but lets the leaf breathe. Use dormant oil emulsion sprays as near blossom time as possible. Dust with ground limestone and sulfur.

Blights and rusts. Plant only resistant varieties. Cut off and burn infected branches. Rake up and burn fallen leaves that are infected.

VEGETABLES

Plant vegetables in soil enriched with compost, manures, or other organic fertilizers. Fast, healthy growth will outrun most vegetable pests. Plant trap crops for known insect pests. These are plants more favored by the insects or ones that come on earlier and lure them away from the main crop (see text for examples).

Insect controls for vegetables will be the same as for fruit trees but there is a specific kind of trichogramma for field crops, *Trichogramma pretiosum*. Twenty-four thousand trichogrammas plus 500 lacewing larvae cost only $7.50. Add a quart of ladybugs and a mantis case or two, and you are well protected.

Don't be too neat too suddenly. Beneficial insects need some cover and food. Leave some nitrogen-fixing legumes around the borders until the main crops are under way.

Bone meal, ground limestone, and sulfur all make vegetables unpalatable to insects. Try dusting cabbage and similar crops with these. (See text for warning on sulfur.)

To combat diabrotica (cucumber beetle), weevils, and some other insects, hold a shallow pan of soapy water or kerosene under the plant and tap it. The pests will drop.

Most eggs are laid on the undersides of vegetable leaves. Run a stick along the row to expose these and pick them off leaves with clusters.

Have places among the vegetables where toads can hide. A loose rock mound, inverted flowerpot, or even boards will serve. Let them dig their own caves and don't hoe them out. A hundred toads will destroy more insect pests than all the sprays in Christendom.

Try interplanting with herbs such as tansy and rue. Nasturtiums are said to repel aphids.

Flea beetles and leafhoppers can be reduced by the use of sticky bands coated with an equal mix of molasses and pine tar.

Large caterpillars, like the tomato hornworm, can be handpicked. If you don't spray, internal parasites will keep them to a minimum.

When all else fails, use the safe botanicals: pyrethrin and rotenone (but be sure there are no poisonous additives in prepared sprays under these names).

ORNAMENTALS

Pot-grown plants may develop severe symptoms of nutritional deficiencies. The symptoms vary from stunted growth, small leaves, and few blooms, to red and yellow blotches between leaf veins. The latter is due to boron deficiency, caused by using only perlite, sand, peat moss, and other inert materials in the mix—these lack both trace elements and major nutrients. Make your mix with compost, well-rotted animal manures, and one of the mild organic fertilizers.

Pots and containers that stand outside in heavy rains can also have all of the soil nutrients washed right through them. This is why planting boxes so often look sickly. Frequent dilute additions of organics such as fish emulsion, bone meal, etc., will keep the plants vigorous. Check the pH or acid-base ratio when plants don't look right. Salts and sometimes acids build up more rapidly in pots and containers than they do in open ground.

In the open garden, mix your plantings. No matter how much you like roses, avoid planting them in a solid mass. Concentrating on one kind of anything will also concentrate that plant's special set of pests and diseases. Mix a few yellow French marigolds, which will make a hot foil for red roses. For something milder, the grey of santolina is a perfect undercover for delicate light-yellow roses. Both of these plants repel insects because of their pungent scents.

In a perennial border, mix in tansy, feverfew, yarrow, and other attractive and aromatic plants. Chives, garlic, and some onions may provide protection or distraction if they are intermixed with vulnerable ornamentals.

Since birds enjoy a mixed planting of shrubs, vines, small trees, and annuals just as much as we do, provide the songbirds with something

extra. Give them a little supplemental food in stormy
times and extra water when it is dry. Most garden
songbirds live on insects.

Plant residues and fallen leaves should be
composted. The heat of decay will destroy
many disease organisms—even viruses. Most fungal
spores and insect eggs will also be destroyed.

A FEW SPECIFICS

Aphids generally collect on the growing tips of
plants. These can be bent down into a bucket
of soapy water, but it must be old-fashioned soap
and not a detergent.

Mealybugs can be destroyed by swabbing them
with kerosene, or rubbing alcohol.

Soil mealybugs and some other soil insects
are controlled by digging in tobacco leavings from
ashtrays. If you don't have these, any cheap
chewing-tobacco will do.

Earwigs can be trapped in short lengths of
discarded plastic garden hose, scattered about the
garden. Early in the morning, tap these into a
bucket of water or paint thinner.

Snails can be killed in great numbers during any
dry period. After a hot spell, water a lawn
thoroughly, late in the evening. After dark take a
flashlight and you will find many of the snails
stretched out soaking up moisture.

Cutworms are often a problem on new plantings.
Try protecting a new plant by setting around
it a cardboard collar or a section cut from a milk
carton.

Can you kill insects with kindness? Sometimes.
Sprinkling bran on potato beetles or cabbage
worms may cause them to overeat. Material rich in
protein, such as cottonseed meal, will cause
some larvae to founder—just as a horse would on
too rich a diet. Even if this tactic doesn't get
them all, it adds fertilizer to your garden soil.

13. Retrospect and Prospect

The gardening methods presented in this book relate to ecology as well as to garden fertility. They are concerned with the creation of a living soil with a high organic content, the use of organic rather than chemical fertilizers when supplements are needed, and the avoidance of chemical poisons in the control of pests and disease. These propositions are as related to one another as are bricks laid in a garden path.

A high organic content in farm and garden soils is desirable, and not only for the mechanical reasons of holding moisture and keeping a good tilth. Added amounts of organic nitrogen increase both the rate of release and the total amount of usable nitrogen available to plants. There is general agreement that the carbonic acid given off in the further decay of organic matter is the stuff that extracts phosphorus and potassium from mineral combinations and makes them available as plant food. This means that the organic matter is needed even by those who garden with chemical fertilizers.

LIVING VERSUS STERILE SOILS

Until the present at least, the concept of a living soil has not been much in favor with the scientists who advise growers and gardeners. Whereas we have argued that a balance of microorganisms in the soil is desirable, many scientists claim that it is a menace. They advocate the burning of agricultural wastes to protect against disease organisms. Each year, 112,000 acres of rice stubble are burned in the counties around California's state capital. In the fall of 1969, the resulting pollution made capital air unbreathable, so something may yet be done about the practice, though for reasons other than our concern for the quality of the soil.

In Oregon's Willamette Valley, some 700,000 tons of straw from grass-seed crops is burned each year. The pollution from this amounts to more than 5,000 tons of solids that blacken the sky and drift down over the city of Eugene. In one day, 183 persons needed medical attention because of this pollution. As an excuse for the practice, John R. Hardison of the United States Department of Agriculture stated that "burning controls hundreds of plant diseases that attack the grass-seed crop, destroys weeds, and is a low-cost way of getting rid of the straw."

Of course, if there really were hundreds of diseases attacking this crop, something is drastically wrong with the methods used. It just might be burning. Burning deprives the soil of its natural processes and of the organic matter that supports a living soil. These are not isolated examples—one single California county

99

reported in 1960 that 41,000 tons of orchard prunings were burned.

Another fact in the depletion of these lands is the vast tonnage of fruit taken off. All of that growth comes out of the same soil each year, and orchards never rest like row crops, so the decades tick away without any organic matter being returned to that soil. Yet we are told by a government publication issued in 1969 that "until means are found for controlling the survival of plant pathogens in the buried wastes, burning will continue to be the only safe way (with respect to plants) of disposing of orchard and vineyard wastes."

Burning is undoubtedly "low-cost"— to the farmer, that is. The solids from agricultural burning are not in themselves as bad as auto exhaust, but they do form nuclei around which industrial and auto fumes collect. The result is truly unbreathable air. Perhaps this issue will be settled in a contest of cost to the farmer versus cost to the public from burning. Probably the pathogen or disease survival is only a public relations argument, in any case.

Although you can start a pot plant in a sterile medium and keep it that way for a short time, there is no possibility of entirely sterilizing an open field. If you could come up with a sterile field, it would be the homesteading target of every organism alive, and there is every likelihood that the first to establish a claim would not be a friend.

The alternative theory is called "dynamic equilibrium," which assumes all manner of living things in the soil. Some of these will be breaking down into organic matter, others will be transforming sulfur into usable plant food. There will also be earthworms and insects. Needless to say, there will also be the organisms that carry plant diseases. In a state of soil equilibrium,

these will be kept in check both by competition and by the antibiotic activities of other soil organisms.

We are all familiar with antibiotics such as penicillin and streptomycin, but there are others that come from soil organisms. One group of microbes related to bacteria, but not the same, are called actinomycetes. Their action against disease is extremely important. In 1967 Dr. Hamao Umezawa published a medical index that required 954 pages simply to list the antibiotic effects of this group of soil organisms. Man is interested in combatting human disease; he would be wise to study further the same effects that have been at work in the soil for ages. There they keep down excesses of certain kinds and insure a healthful medium for growing plants.

COMPOSTING AGAIN

When great buildups of plant disease actually do occur, composting is more effective than burning. If you have ever built a large fire, you may have noticed the remarkable fact that nothing at all will grow on the scorched patch for several years. Composting, on the other hand, is a very mild burn. It eliminates some microbes, while those that work at decay and transformation are untouched. After the first heat, even earthworms are unharmed. What is left are available plant foods. The heat of composting will not have killed all weed seeds, plant diseases and pests, but it will have attained a balance. This is the same combination that works on a forest floor or a good meadow. There will not be perfection, but nature tends to balance lives and kinds.

Even the heat from a forest fire or a brush fire is selective in intensity—it skims over some parts and merely touches others. This is unlike man's disposal of wastes by burning. Earlier in this book composting was considered in terms of methods used; but here it is considered again as an alternative to other methods of disposing of wastes, and also in relation to the wider ecology that includes man and his place in a livable world.

Livability and stability are very much the same kind of thing. There are always changes, by the day or by the decade, but the new relationships still have to attain some kind of balance. In terms of soil, it is well to remember that Europeans have farmed the same land for two thousand years or more. We, on the other hand, have farmed the eastern part of the country for perhaps two hundred years, and the western part for half that time. Some soils, such as the cotton lands around Dallas, are already depleted, while everywhere we are faced with unbearable pollution. These problems arise together and they can probably be solved together.

WILL SYNTHETIC FERTILIZERS SAVE US?

During the last half-century, farmers have increasingly relied on chemical fertilizers to keep up the fertility of their land. Some years ago I took a course in floriculture, and one lecture naturally dealt with fertilizers. The instructor had heard of organic methods but dismissed these quite simply: there just isn't enough manure anymore, he said, while the supply of chemical fertilizers is endless.

As it turns out now, he had his truths reversed. Native sources of commercial fertilizer are diminishing rapidly. The U.S. Bureau of Mines published a circular in 1969 (#8418) entitled *A Statistical Analysis of U.S. Demand for Phosphate, Rock, Potash and Nitrogen.* This publication makes good reading, particularly when you read between the lines. What is interesting here is not the *demand* but the *supply* of these three basic fertilizing elements.

There are mineable supplies of phosphate rock in only four states in the Northwest and three in the East. According to the report, the supplies in Tennessee will be exhausted in from twelve to twenty-five years; those in Florida will last from forty to fifty years; in North Carolina the mines should be able to turn out this material for another thirty-five to forty years. In the West the reserves are a little greater, but tonnage-wise this entire reserve amounts to only a third more than the animal wastes that are produced every single year.

Super-phosphate and triple-phosphate are made by treating mined phosphate rock with sulfuric acid and phosphoric acid. The latter gives a product that is 52 percent phosphate (P_2O_5). That is the kind of material that makes farmers complain about the "shot in the arm" effect of commercial fertilizers. Super-phosphate is the milder combination with sulfuric acid.

The second of the big three elements in commercial fertilizer is potash. Potash is extracted from bedded material in New Mexico and from brine in California and Utah. According to the same circular, "if U.S. domestic sources were to furnish all supplies of potash to U.S. users, the New Mexico ore would be depleted by 1980." The supply would then come from brine operations, and these would be depleted by the year 2000. The nitrogen of the air is extracted, in a roundabout way, by growing plant life, and it can also be made synthetically. Hence, it will not be in short supply.

The thought that native supplies of phosphorus and potash will be exhausted within a generation need not be alarming. These are mineable supplies used for commercial fertilizer. Most soils contain a goodly amount of both, brought up from decaying rocks beneath the topsoil. To replenish what is extracted, we can add animal and vegetable wastes. Both bone meal and chicken manure are high in phosphates, and wood ashes contain potash. Farmyard manure also contains enough potash to keep the soil supplied, and this is an item we come to next.

SOLID WASTES

This is a rather new term to cover everything that society doesn't want, or thinks it doesn't want. Urban garbage, food processing wastes, agricultural and industrial wastes—these we want to get rid of. Surprisingly enough, it is not used cans and bottles or discarded cars that provide the bulk of the problem.

In May, 1969, the Office of Science and Technology prepared for the President a report entitled *Solid Waste Management.* It turns out that our discards are the other side of the coin from our dwindling supplies of phosphorus and potash for commercial fertilizers. In fact, the problem of solid wastes reads very much like assembling material for a compost pile.

We have too much unwanted animal and vegetable waste. First of all, there is too much old-fashioned manure. As the study puts it: "Domestic animals produce over 1 billion tons of fecal wastes a year and over 400 million tons of liquid waste. Used bedding, paunch manure from abattoirs, and dead carcasses make the total annual production of animal wastes close to 2 billion tons."

Now you might think that Farmer Jones puts all of that manure back into the soil. If times hadn't changed, there would be no need for a Presidential commission. What has happened is that in the last generation, dairy, poultry, and cattle feeding operations have left the farm and moved to the suburbs. According to this same study, "As much as 50 percent of animal wastes is generated in concentrated growing operations close to urban areas." A dairy herd of 400 milk cows produces 14 tons of solid waste daily. In the suburbs, this "waste" is likely to be flushed into streams and rivers.

The agricultural branch of the University of California at Davis set up a "task force" to prepare a "position paper" on animal solid waste. The phrases are clichés denoting urgency. On the happy side they came up with the opinion that this state doesn't really have 22 million tons of animal wastes each year, but a mere 16 million tons (undehydrated). But on the cheerless side they also found that manure "has become a cost item instead of a demand product, especially in view of cheaper, easier to handle chemical fertilizers."

This "task force," with its destroyers up front and its battle wagons held in the rear, comes up with a solution—burning! Burning? Yes, but "unconventional burning." They realize that we can't put up with much more smog, so they suggested a nonexistent furnace which might convert manure into electric power. That will doubtless take another task force from the engineering department some time to design and perfect.

VEGETABLE WASTES

As we build our hypothetical compost pile, vegetable material appears next on the waste list. The President's solid-waste report states, "Major agricultural crop wastes amounted to 550 million tons a year." That is a tidy sum and not all of it is burned or left in the field. Food processing, like livestock, has moved toward the suburbs and cities. In processing corn alone, about 30 percent of the weight is lost at the cannery, not in the fields. Probably you have seen local fruit and vegetable processing plants pumping this excess "sludge" into local creeks and rivers.

Animal and vegetable wastes are valuable when composted, but if they are pumped into streams, rivers, bays, and lakes, these concentrations are totally destructive to aquatic ecology. That is doubly bad in that it pollutes the waters and deprives the land of rightful returns.

It seems transparently clear that the best way to dispose of these millions of tons of unwanted animal and vegetable wastes is to compost them on a grand scale. In that process, weight shrinks considerably, and the end product is a dry crumbly material that is easy to handle. If we think in terms of the generation after our own and those that follow, there is really no alternative other than returning this extracted richness to the soil.

WHY DON'T WE COMPOST ON A LARGE SCALE?

Short-term economic profit is the answer. To quote the same study once more:

"Within the concept of solid waste management, no special merit is given to one system of processing waste over another. Composting is one of many processing techniques and as such it is given preference only when it is the most economical system or whenever society is willing to pay an additional price for returning wastes that are compatible to the environment."

Actually the question is not one of awarding merit badges but one of handing on a fertile soil for future generations.

Then, too, one should take a second look at that word "processing." This seems to suggest that we have alternatives to large-scale composting, whereas alternative modes of processing really consist only of burning or dumping. Burning can become more sophisticated, and dumping can take place in more remote spots, such as deserts and outer oceans. Either way is going to be at least as expensive as composting.

SHOULD COMPOSTING BE SUBSIDIZED?

Indeed it will have to be because to date no private businessman has been able to set up an operation of this type that would return a profit. But that fact is not surprising since a city doesn't make money on its garbage—it pays! It is difficult to start a private business, and when the concept is new, the difficulties are extreme. We have, after all, poured billions into subsidizing tobacco, rice, cotton, peanuts, and sundry grains.

Some of these funds could be devoted to a pioneer project in mass composting, and with initial help the process could be made to pay. By the turn of this century, the population will be a matter of all elbows rather than elbow-room. Untold billions of tons more in food and waste will have been removed from the soil. A thoughtful step or two in the direction of conservation by large-scale composting would be certain to pay a handsome return in future soil fertility.

For the present, any environmental gardener can take advantage of these wastes that are going to waste. But gardeners worth their composts will also take part in conservation movements and also make sure that those things politicians promise in this field pass from talk to reality. Conservation is merely a broader application of the principles advocated by organic gardening.

Both movements agree that we should destroy as little of our environment as possible, whether this is life in the soil or wildlife above it. We also agree that when something is withdrawn, something will have to be put in. This is a physical fact as well as an aesthetic and moral consideration. We would like to see the world remain as a garden or a pleasant field, and that prospect is now in doubt, even for our own generation.

103

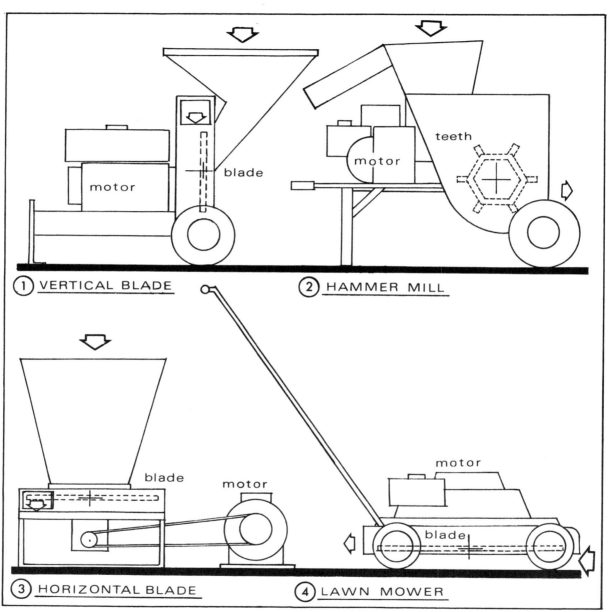

① VERTICAL BLADE — blade, motor

② HAMMER MILL — teeth, motor

③ HORIZONTAL BLADE — blade, motor

④ LAWN MOWER — motor, blade

Chopping machines. *Drawing by Adrián Martínez*

Appendix

SHREDDERS AND CHOPPERS

There are several different types of shredders and choppers. The simplest and cheapest consists of whirling rotary blades—much like your lawn mower—but set in the bottom of a hopper. Some models can even be attached to a lawn mower and use its power. This is a good system for chopping light material.

Another machine works like a tiller—rotating blades chop matter into the soil. This is good, but cannot be used for making a compost heap. There is also a powerful chopper which uses a vertical blade. One can think of an airplane propeller in motion, with material being fed through it.

Most choppers are based on the hammermill principle. This is a powerful and serviceable design familiar in hay choppers and the "hogs" that are used by road crews to grind up tree trimmings. It consists of a set of whirling claws that work against a screen. Interchangeable screens of different size determine how fine the material will be ground. In powerful models of this type of machine, limbs as large as ¾ inch can be reduced to a compostable pulp.

Since outside burning is being prohibited in many areas, a powerful machine can also be valuable in taking care of all your trash problems. On the other hand, the larger machines are expensive. Think carefully about your requirements, and send for several catalogs before making a decision. You will want to choose a machine that is not too weak or too strong for the work you want to do. Remember that a machine that weighs 42 pounds is not going to have the same capacity as one that weighs 200 pounds.

Most shredders are on wheels so that they can be moved from place to place, and that is almost essential unless you have an extremely small garden.

Some of the manufacturers who make models suitable for home gardens follow:

M. A. Johnson
Route 5, Box 447
Taylorsville, N. Carolina 28681
A single blade, lightweight machine that can be attached to a mower

Kemp Shredder Co.
P.O. Box 975
Erie, Pennsylvania 16512
Hammermill type; many models from an inexpensive "Shredette" to garden models in the $220 plus range to very heavy duty types

Lindig Mfg. Corporation
1875 West Country Road C.
St. Paul, Minnesota 55113
Highspeed hammermill

Red Cross Manufacturing Corp.
Box 111
Bluffton, Indiana 46714
Has single blade, vertical and attached directly to shaft of motor, working against rigid shredding knives; there are large and small models (3 and 6 hp); lightweight

Roto-Hoe Company
Newbury, Ohio 44065
Hammermill type; many models; specializing in units that will fit to basic power unit—can be chopper, tiller, snow plow, etc.

Royer Foundry & Machine Co.
185 Pringle Street
Kingston, Pennsylvania 18704
Capacities from 5 to 100 cubic yards an hour

Troy-built Roto Tillers
102nd Street & 9th Avenue
Troy, New York 12182
New model rototiller combines the action of chopping with tilling; matter is first chopped and then turned under

W-W Grinder Corp.
2957 North Market
Wichita, Kansas 67219
Hammermill type; many models including large ones; garden models begin at a modest price ($111 minus power); about twice that for a larger garden model with power

Winona Attrition Mill Co.
1009 West Fifth Street
Winona, Minnesota 55987
"Speedy" shredders have from 16 to 32 hinged knives; they are lightweight, low cost and easy to handle

EARTHWORMS

Earthworms are comparatively easy to raise, so there are many more sources for them than for control-insects. Probably you can find a local grower in the classified ads or in the phone book. A few places for mail-order earthworms:

Brazos Worm Farms
Route 9
Waco, Texas 76705

Bronwood Worm Gardens
Bronwood, Georgia 31726

Cottage Industries Northwest
Burley, Washington 98322

Oakhaven Enterprises
Cedar Hills, Texas 75104

Andrew Peoples
R.D. #1
Lansdale, Pennsylvania 19445

Sunada Enterprises
Box 362
Parlier, California 93648

BENEFICIAL INSECTS FOR BIOLOGICAL CONTROL

Raising insects, or even gathering them, for biological control use is difficult. As a result, there is a great deal of specialization. Most firms try to work with more than one control insect but are often short in supply of the second group. Some of the basic suppliers are:

Bio-Control Co.
Rt. 2, Box 2397
Auburn, California 95603
Ladybug beetles gathered in the Sierras from winter colonies; two species; sometimes mantis cases

Ecological Insect Services
15075 W. California Avenue
Kerman, California 93630
Consultation and control for both farms and gardens; sells retail

Gothard, Inc.
P.O. Box 370
Canutillo, Texas 79835
Specializes in trichogramma wasps

Mincemoyer's Nursery
R.D. 5, Box 379
New Prospect Road
Jackson, New Jersey 08527
Mantis egg cases, both native and Chinese

Rincon Insectary Inc.
1462 Callens Road
Ventura, California 93003
Raises control insects for farm work

Schnoor's Sierra Bug Co.
P.O. Box 114
Rough and Ready, California 95975
Ladybugs only

The Vitova Co., Inc.
Biological Control Division
P.O. Box 745
Rialto, California 92376
Lacewings (larvae or young adults); two kinds of trichogramma; parasites for fly maggots and armyworms

SOIL TEST KITS AND SOIL ACIDITY TAPES

The House Plant Corner
P.O. Box 810
Oxford, Maryland 21654

Indiana Botanic Gardens Inc.
Hammond, Indiana 46325

LaMotte Chemical Products Co.
Chestertown, Maryland 21620

Nichols Garden Nursery
Pacific North
Albany, Oregon 97321

Organic Gardening & Farming Magazine
Emmaus, Pennsylvania 18049

Park Seed Company
Greenwood, South Carolina 29646

Sudbury Laboratory Inc.
Box 1076
Sudbury, Massachusetts 01776

NETTING AND TRAPS AGAINST BIRD DAMAGE
Animal Repellents
P.O. Box 168
Griffin, Georgia 30223
Netting

Apex Mills, Inc.
49 West 37th Street
New York, New York 10018
Netting

LIVE TRAPS FOR BIRDS AND ANIMALS
Havahart
148 Water Street
Ossining, New York 10562
Live animal traps

Johnson's
Box 13
Waverly, Kentucky 42462
Sparrow and starling traps; also animal traps

TRAPS FOR INSECTS
Agrilite Systems, Inc.
404 Barringer Building
Columbia, South Carolina

Aquacide—IMS Corporation
Albuquerque, New Mexico

Ray Collier
2499 Greenway Street, South
St. Petersburg, Florida 33712

D-vac Co.
P.O. Box 2095
Riverside, California 92506

Insect-O-Lite Company
1925 Queen City Avenue
Cincinnati, Ohio

Stickem—Michael and Pelton
Oakland, California

The Tanglefoot Company
314 Straight Avenue, S.W.
Grand Rapids, Michigan

HERBS FOR REPELLING INSECTS
Merry Gardens
Camden, Maine 04843

Nichols Garden Nursery
1190 North Pacific Highway
Albany, Oregon 97321

Sunnybrook Farms Nursery
9448 Mayfield Road
Chesterland, Ohio 44026

BOTANICALS
Desert Herb Tea Co.
736 Darling Street
Ogden, Utah

Indiana Botanic Gardens, Inc.
Hammond, Indiana 46325

PYRETHRUM
Agra Industries, Ltd.
355 Lexington Avenue
New York, New York 10017

Chemical Compounding Co.
1459 Third Street
Oakland, California 94607

McLaughlin Gormley King Co.
1715 5th Street, S.E.
Minneapolis, Minnesota 55414

Pyrethrum Information Center
Room 423
744 Broad Street
Newark, New Jersey 07102

Thompson & Morgan
London Road
Ipswich-Suffolk
England

BIRD HOUSE KITS AND PLANS
Audubon Workshop
Glenview, Illinois 60025

SOME NATIONAL CONSERVATION GROUPS

There are organizations dedicated to protecting our natural heritage in the world around us. Often their aims are similar to ours as organic gardeners, and we can join together. Some of these organizations are listed below. There are many more local groups in which you will find friends and information.

California Tomorrow
681 Market Street
San Francisco, California 94105

Friends of the Earth
30 East 42nd Street
New York, New York 10017

Friends of the Earth
451 Pacific Avenue
San Francisco, California 94133

National Audubon Society
1130 Fifth Avenue
New York, New York 10028

National Wildlife Federation
1412 Sixteenth Street, N.W.
Washington, D.C. 20036

Nature Conservancy
215 Market Street
San Francisco, California

Sierra Club
1050 Mills Tower
San Francisco, California 94104

The Isaak Walton League of America
1326 Waukegan Road
Glenview, Illinois 60025

The Wilderness Society
729 Fifteenth Street, N.W.
Washington, D.C. 20005

SOME RECOMMENDED BOOKS

Pesticides and Their Effects
Carson, Rachel. *Silent Spring.* Crest, 1969 (paper).
De Bell, Garrett. *The Environmental Handbook.* Ballantine / Friends of the Earth, 1970 (paper).
Rudd, Robert L. *Pesticides and the Living Landscape.* University of Wisconsin Press, 1966 (paper).

Soil
Balfour, E. B. *The Living Soil.* Devin-Adair, 1952.
Waksman, S. A. *Humus.* Williams & Wilkins.
————. *Soil Microbiology.* 1952 (o.p.)

Composting
Howard, Sir Albert. *An Agricultural Testament.* Oxford, 1940.
Rodale, J. *Complete Book of Composting.* Rodale Press, Emmaus, Pa. 18049.
Seifert, Alwin. *Compost.* Faber & Faber.

Earthworms
Barrett, Thomas J. *Earthworms, Their Intensive Propagation and Use in Biological Soil-Building.* Earthmaster Publications, 1952.
Darwin, Charles. *Darwin on Humus and the Earthworm.* Faber & Faber, 1956.

Insects
Brooklyn Botanic Garden. "Handbook on Biological Control of Plant Pests."
Lutz, Frank E. *Field Book of Insects.* New York, 1948.
U. S. Department of Agriculture. "Biological Control of Insect Pests," Technical Bulletin #1139. 1956.
————. *Insects.* Yearbook for 1952.

Birds
Baker, et. al. *The Audubon Guide to Attracting Birds.* Doubleday.
Lemmon, Robert S. *How to Attract Birds.* American Garden Guild.
McElroy, Thomas P., Jr. *Handbook of Attracting Birds.* Knopf.
Peterson, Roger Tory. *A Field Guide to the Birds; A Field Guide to Western Birds; A Field Guide to the Birds of Texas and Adjacent States.* Houghton Mifflin Co.

Index